Hidden Symbolism In The COUNCIL OF THE SEVEN LIGHTS
An Annotated Edition

George W. Van Tassel
Kenneth Arnold

SAUCERIAN PUBLISHER

ISBN: 9781736731420

© 2021, Saucerian Publisher

Al rights reserved. No part of this publication maybe reproduced, translate, store in a retrieval system, or transmitted in any form or by any means, electronic, mechanical, photocopying, recording or otherwise, without prior written permision from the publisher.

George Van Tassel and the Integratron

Prologue

George Van Tassel was an American author and ufologist once claimed to have been in contact with an extraterrestrial from Venus. He was a controversial figure in the annals of ufology.

Van Tassel was born in Jefferson, Ohio in 1910, and grew up in a fairly prosperous middle-class family. He finished high school in the 10th grade and held a job at a small municipal airport near Cleveland; he also acquired a pilot's license. At age 20, he moved to California, where at first he worked as an automobile mechanic at a garage owned by an uncle. While pumping gas at the garage, he met Frank Critzer, an eccentric loner who claimed to be working a mine somewhere near Giant Rock, a 7-story boulder near Landers, California. Frank Critzer was a German immigrant trying to make a living in the desert as a prospector. During World War II, Critzer was under suspicion as a German spy and was killed during a police siege at the Rock in 1942. Upon receiving news of Critzer's death, Van Tassel applied for a lease of the small abandoned airport near Giant Rock from the Bureau of Land Management, and was eventually given a Federal Government contract to develop and maintain the airstrip.

Van Tassel was an accomplished aircraft mechanic and flight inspector who worked for various firms between 1930 and 1947 before retiring to the desert. In 1947, Van Tassel left Southern California's booming aerospace industry to live in the desert with his family. At first, he lived a simple existence in the rooms Frank Critzer had dug out under Giant Rock. Van Tassel eventually built a new home, a cafe, a gas station, a store, a small airstrip, and a ranch beside the Rock.

He rose to prominence as a key figure of interest in 1953 after claiming that he had been awoken one night by an alien from Venus named Solgonda. The being allegedly invited him aboard its spacecraft where Van Tassel was telepathically gifted the plans for a device called the "Integratron" which was said to be capable of rejuvenating the human body.

Van Tassel began constructing the Integratron in 1954 in "an intersection of powerful geomagnetic forces that, when focused by the unique geometry of the building, will concentrate and amplify the energy required for cell rejuvenation". The construction costs were partly paid for by an annual series of successful UFO conventions, the Giant Rock Spacecraft Conventions, which continued for nearly 25 years. The main structure's construction was complete circa 1959, but Van Tassel continued to work on the device until his sudden death in 1978.

According to Van Tassel, the Integratron's workings rely on the generation of strong "intermittent magnetic fields" resulting in the generation of plasma in the form of a coronal discharge and negative air ionization inside the building. The Integratron is based on the Multiple Wave Oscillator invented by Georges Lakhovsky. The Multiple Wave Oscillator is a combination of a high voltage Tesla coil and a split-ring resonator that generates ultra wideband electromagnetic frequencies. Van Tassel speculated that electromagnetism affects biological cells, and believed that every biological cell has a unique resonant electromagnetic frequency. According to van Tassel, the generation of strong ultra wideband EMF by the Integratron "resonates" with the cell's frequency and "recharges" the cellular structure as if it were an electrical battery. Van Tassel claimed that human cells "rejuvenated" while inside the structure. Van Tassel also claimed the Integratron is intentionally constructed atop a powerful geomagnetic anomaly and its construction is entirely of non-ferromagnetic materials, the equivalent to a modern radome.

Saucerian Publisher was founded with the mission of promoting books in Science Fiction, Paranormal, and the Occult. Our vision is to preserve the legacy of literary history by reprint editions of books which have already been exhausted or are difficult to obtain. Our goal is to help readers, educators and researchers by bringing back original publications that are difficult to find at reasonable price, while preserving the legacy of universal knowledge. This book is an authentic reproduction of the original printed text. Because this book is culturally important, we have made available as part of our commitment to protect, preserve and promote knowledge in the world. 'This title was originally published in 1958.

In his book of 1958: *The Council of Seven Lights,* George van Tassel produced a compilation of communications describing a reality that many of us are not familiar with. Much of the information is complex and was not easily understood. The subject matters include the cycling of twelve densities, the progressed evolution of planets, and the connection between gravity and electricity. He takes the reader far beyond our atmosphere to give technical data on the lines of energy, the conditions of space. He describes polarity, its positive and negative aspects, and applies theory to fact so the reader can understand every point he makes. The beginning of all creation has the same meaning as the ending of all creation, for all things have always existed and always will exist. Everything anyone has ever been or will ever be, he is now. This is a truth often overlooked in man's search for understanding. He forgets God was all there was, and therefore all there is now or will ever be. Van Tassel writes that religion and science are the same thing, the only difference being that they are two opposite viewpoints. Just as a wall is a wall regardless of which side one stands on, so are science and religion, life itself. According to Van Tassel, the Bible is an accurate history of events repeating themselves in cycles. He says there are predictions referring to spaceships throughout the Bible, among them the prophecy that there will be a day when the ships will come to take the people who are ready, leaving those who are not prepared to face the cataclysmic destruction inevitably approaching.

This book explains the vortices of the human body that are responsible for the reasons that certain individuals affect one so strongly on meeting, a violent, a strong attraction without apparent cause, and also explain a person's effect on each others. In The *Council of Seven Lights*, the reader will ind many absorbing facets of knowledge - new data on atmospheric conditions, further information about space ships, and for the searcher who desires more understanding of the greater pattern of life, a philosophy well worth studying.

Original text with almost 100 annotations. This title is the most comprehensive study on Van Tassel ever published, and illuminates every dimension of George Van Tassel's hidden symbolism behind his writings.

Kenneth Arnold
Saucerian Publisher, 2021

TABLE OF CONTENTS

Chapter		Page
	INTRODUCTION	1
One	THE MISSING LINK	7
	Drawing 1	13
Two	INVISIBLE GEARS	20
	Drawing 2	22
Three	THE SUN OF GOD	34
	Drawing 3	37
Four	TRINITY OF INFINITY	51
Five	UNSEEN SCALES	59
	Drawing 4	60
Six	THE ANGELS OF SPACE	68
Seven	PRODIGAL MOTHER	80
	Drawing 5 (Between 83 & 84)	
	Drawing 6 (Between 91 & 92)	
	Drawing 7 (Between 97 & 98)	
Eight	METHUSELAH'S TOY	110
	Drawing 8	111
Nine	THE SWORD OF DAMOCLES	117
Ten	THE FALSE CHARIOT	127
	NOTES	136
	ADDENDUM	209

INTRODUCTION

THE COUNCIL[3] OF SEVEN[1] LIGHTS[2,66]

INTRODUCTION

Para-psychology[8] has proven that the transmission and reception of thought is possible and a scientific fact.

The information in this book is the result of a developed ability to awaken the nearly dormant consciousness to thoughts existing throughout time.

Nothing can be thought of that has not been thought of before. The principles of radio, television, electricity, flying, and of all modem things, existed in the time of Plato and Columbus. All of the principles of everything that can ever be already exist in the infinity of <u>Universal Mind</u>[4].

The ability to penetrate Mind[5] requires practice. In practicing the act of awareness I found that Intelligence exists throughout the Universe[7].

My first contact with the organized Intelligences of other places revealed that the Intelligence manifested on the Earth[10] is in the kindergarten stages. My penetration into the superconscious[6] mind[5] revealed an eternal record of infinite laws.

Thinking is not something one does. Thinking is the act of becoming aware of what already exists. One does not try to

INTRODUCTION

think to become aware. One[9] only has to remove his own thoughts and. Then the Universal Mind[4] rushes in to fill the void.

The introduction of any new thought is usually accepted by those who understand its potentialities, and rejected by those who do not comprehend its portent. This often leads to controversy, which is the needed stimulant that brings individuals to the use of their own thought power.

This book is not written with the intention to present anything radically new to the reader. It is written to revive that which has become nearly dormant within his individual power of conception.

One[9] would be utterly foolish to try Ito explain a subject using scientific explanations to another who is not interested in or doesn't understand scientific terms. It would be equally unimpressive to appeal to one from the religious viewpoint if he were not interested in religion[13].

My desire in presenting this book is to pass on that which makes sense to my reasoning faculties, in the hope that others can gain something of lasting value from it.

The materialism of the present society of the masses is evidence that even the most unreligious of individuals has a desire to worship something; so he worships matter. The materialists think they are the more advanced people in an otherwise scientifically ignorant society.

The most devout religionists[13] lean the other way and believe

INTRODUCTION

their heavenly point of view is the correct way. Actually both are wrong and both are right; from a neutral point of view.

I am attempting to present this book from the middle viewpoint. If it appears lthat I am leaning one way or the other, the reader may take into· account that perhaps he is basing his opinion on his own tendency to lean one way or the other. Now, the best way to really understand anything is to examine your own opinion from the opposite point of view.

This book is an attempt to present to science and religion the facts that each are integral parts of the other, and both are the same ONE[9] from opposite concepts. A wall is a wall regardless of from which side one looks at it. On one side of this wall is written the history land achievements of science, and on the other side one can read the records of the various religions[13].

There is only the one principle of creation, but there are many roads to finding this grand principle.

Religion[13] presents its *many* roads to the people; each sect presenting its approach as the only one, with the fanatic condemnation of all other religious roads. The many divisions of science each profess their findings as the eternal verities.

Religion[13] presents God[11,12] as the <u>Infinite Being</u>[12]; and science presents the manifestations of God[11,12] which have been recorded with the five senses.

In the unthinkable vastness of the infinite universe the Earth[10]

INTRODUCTION

is only a tiny speck of matter, inhabited by parasites called humans. The people depend upon the Earth[10] for their sustenance the same as any parasite depends upon its host for life.

Religion[13] is the art of *living* now. A true religionist knows how to live without infringing upon the rightful living of others. The professors of religion propound spirit as something you become after your death. Actually the spiritt of you is here now and your god is determnined by the way you live in the flesh body so as to manifest spirit now, here on Earth[10].

The consciousness of every individual contains all of the records of every act and personality that the individual has ever done, or been.

To admit that many of the thoughts I received were given by other identities would be true. Yet the further truth is that I have been all of these other identities.

Reincarnation[13] is a misnomer. All that one has ever been or will ever be, he is now. Everyone has always existed since the creation[16a].

Whether one accepts the limits of one life span here on the Earth[10], or this life and a hereafter somewhere else is of no concern. One[9] cannot honestly believe in a hereafter without believing in a "before".

This schoolroom on the Earth[10] is only a brief experience in

INTRODUCTION

eternal Life.

One[9] must first understand himself, then he may understand his fellowman. If this is accomplished then one is at the doorway of understanding God[11,12].

*0 man, you have made laws to avoid using My
Laws.*

*Confusion, chaos, and war are the results of man's
ideas, opinion, and assumptions.*

*Light alone is the essence of Truth;
Truth alone is the essence of Wisdom;
Wisdom is the essence of Knowledge;
Knowledge is the essence of Life.*

*Only through Knowledge can man express Wisdom
in action.*

*I have given man Life that he might demonstrate
My Knowledge through action and Wisdom.*

*I extend the concentration of My Light to those
who are demonstrating My Laws.*

*0 man, in living My life, in breathing My breath,
establish within yourself the solidarity, the contentment,
the bliss of living rightly; that I may know,
that I may feel the glorious pulsation of the Being
of you. In speaking My words, let them ring clear,
let them be dear and near to you that others may
understand. Realize, I am not the expression of self;*

INTRODUCTION

I am only the boundless unselfish utterances of the heart and the Soul that sees Me in others. None can bring about the workings of My Laws, unless first they have established their right within My Light.

Reach not for golden prizes of desire, for they shall reflect the Light. Look not into the mirrors of space, for eyes that see are blind to Me. And though the Prize be golden, My light does not reflect. Express the Being of Me in life, extend Me in the action that I may feel the thrill of doing for another whose need is great, that I may know success in manifesting you to bring about the Me in others, that their eyes may see through thee to Me not reflection, not illusion, but the purity, the reality I have instilled within the you of Me.

CHAPTER ONE THE MISSING LINK

CHAPTER ONE

THE MISSING LINK

"In the beginning God[11] created the heaven and the earth[10]." (Gen.1:1). This creation[16a] was a part of the continuously evolving creation throughout the universe. Each instant that passes new things are being made, new phases of life unfold, to live in ever progressing <u>cycles of rebirth</u>[14].

As related above God[11] made heaven before Earth[10]. In these heavens of the sky He had already created Man. On many planets in many other solar systems, and on other planets in this sollar system, Man was developed through thousands of years, even before the Earth[10] was habitable.

Man was created (Gen. 1: 27), *he did not evolve from the lower animals.*

However, he was not created on the Earth[10]. Man was created throughout millions of solar systems; to serve as the instrument of God's[11] doing. Anyone who contends that this planet is the only one occupied by intelligent life forms, does not accept God[11] in His infinite completeness. His narrow mind has placed a limit on His ability to perform His creations[16a].

Adam was not a single man. The <u>Adamic *race of Man*</u>[15] was

CHAPTER ONE THE MISSING LINK

the first people to inhabit the Earth[10]. This is confirmed in Gen. 1:27 where the race of Man, in the original creation, is described as "male and female". In Gen. 1:28 the scripture relates how "God[11] blessed them". This is plural, not *him,* but *them.* And God[11] said unto *them* (the Adamic race[15,] both male and female) "be fruitful, and multiply". This all happens before Eve is ever mentioned. Thus the Adamic race[15] is established on Earth[10].

Then God[11] finished His work of creation in regard to Man. He had also finished the creation of the *heavens* and the *Earth*[10] (Gen. 2: 1) and all the host of *them.* This means all the beings who occupied the Earth and the *heavens.* So God[11] "ended His work" and rested. (Gen. 2:2,3).

Can this be that God[11] ended His work, and still no mention of Eve? Yes, the Bible is accurate on God's[11] beginning of His creations[16a].

Then comes the *summary* of the creation[16a]. This is where people are led into confusion. For the first time God[11] is left out of the picture and we have a "Lord God[11]" (Heb.-Jehovah Elohim). This *character* was one of the Adamic race[15] who was in the colony that had been landed here by spacecraft. The men of the Adamic race[15] did not bring their women with them when they first landed on Earth[10]. .

CHAPTER ONE THE MISSING LINK

The Lord God[11] brings Eve into the picture, not the Creator[16]. The Lord God[11] said that the Adamic men[15] were lonesome. (Gen. 2: 18). Then the Lord God[11] pops Eve out of a rib after one of their people fell into a deep sleep. (Gen. 2 : 21,22). God[11] brings about the creation[16] of people through birth everywhere in the universe, not by making women out of men's ribs.

The *race* of Eve was the highest form of lower animal life on this planet. *They were not apes,* but they were also not the race of Man, *created by God*[11].

Next comes the story of Adam[27], Eve, and the apple. (Gen. 3 : 1-7). This son of the Adamic race[15] of Man blamed the woman, and the woman blamed the serpent[17]. The poor serpent didn't have anyone to blame.

One of the true species of Man, as God[11] *created* the Adamic race[15], mated with an animal. There is no violation of God's[11] law in man mating with woman *after his own kind.* Adam's[27] violation of the law was not in "eating the apple"; it was in eating the *wrong* apple.

God[11] created every creature ,after its own kind (Gen. 1:11,12 and 21, 22), but one of the race of Man mated with an animal of the Earth[10] and *crossed blood.*

This is where Man became *hu-man.* Eve[23] gave birth to

CHAPTER ONE THE MISSING LINK

Cain[21] and Abel[22]. She didn't know who the (Creator[16] was, so she said, "I have gotten a man from the Lord[11]" (Gen. 4: 1), thinking the Lord[11] was the <u>Adamic man</u>[15] who was her mate.

When Cain[21] killed Abel[22] he revealed the animal nature of his mother[10]. He started the practice of murder, that has expanded to a point now where people can vaporize thousands of others with atomic and hydrogen bombs. Thatt is why the people of the Earth[10] are called humans. The Adamic sons[15] of God[11] knew the tiger as a killer among beasts. The name for tiger[24] was "Hu"[24a].

Most of the people on the Earth[10] today are crossbreed descendants of the true Adamic sons[15] of God[11], as originally created, and the animal race of Eve[23]. That is why you have an earthly, dense, animal body, and an inner body of created reality as God[11] made *You*.

The truly created men and women of the <u>Adamic race</u>[15] of man have been watching the people on the Earth[10] for thousands of years.

This "siva-lization" (from Shiva[19], Hindu god of destruction) of humans has expanded the science of destruction to the . point of crisis. The nations having atomic bombs have enough to wipe out all living things on the Earth[10]. The animal of Eve[23] is in power.

CHAPTER ONE THE MISSING LINK

The Adamic race[15] of Man has brought "nullifier" ships[18] into the Earth's[10] thin film of breathable atmosphere. We call them *green fireballs*. They have nullified concentrations of atomic radiation that were in our atmosphere. They feel responsible for the fact that one of their people started this destructive cycle on the Earth[10] .You have a choice to make. You either accept the Creator's[16] Adamic[15] constructive part of you, or you recognize the physical *hu-man's* destructive influence of the Eve[23] ancestry.

The <u>Adamic race</u>[15] of Man typifies the combination of spirit and substance into form. The many *forms* of life; fish, birds, reptiles, insects, animals, and humans all change with environment and breeding. The human race is a degenerate species of Man, as a result of following the bestial tendencies.

Matter and spirit are the same thing, only in opposite manifestation. Matter is energy (spirit) condensed and energy is matter in solution. Each is polarized throughout infinite space and both follow a pattern of forms.

Space[18] is the infinite ocean of Intelligence (Creative Spirit), or the Creator[16] at rest. This balanced Intelligence manifests through all creations[16a]. In order to manifrest *motion* the *energies* must be unbalanced.

No thing or condition in God's[11] universe is without contrast in duality. For every up there's a down, <u>for every white there's a black, for every night there's a day</u>[25].

CHAPTER ONE THE MISSING LINK

Anyone who has climbed the "tree of knowledge"[20]_ can see that it has two sides, no matter in which direction one looks. This is not because the tree knows one side froin another; it's because the man in the top of it has two sides, his right · and. left.

God [11] made everying in duality so He should remain at rest in the middle; God [11] is peace .

Jesus said "My Father and I are one". That was because he recognized no rich or poor, no boundaries or colors, no church or religions at was because he remained neutral at a division point between the contrasting dualitiies. Jesus didn't take sides with anyone. Actually *you* shouldn't take either side take God's[11] course down the middle.

A fire can warm you or destroy you. Cold [25] is desirable in a refrigerator but not when it makes one uncomfortable. Speed is required to get somewhere fast, but its momentum can kill you if you lose control of it.

Atomic energy is a death force. Its radiation can kill you without a bomb being dropped. In commercial use for power it is as deadly as when it is used in bombs.

Fission or fusion of atoms, or their isotopes, on a planet are not as God[11] intended. God[11] created suns[26] to operate their reactions by the principles of fission and fusion. He also placed the planets far enough away from the suns so there would be no harmful effects from their waste products.

CHAPTER ONE THE MISSING LINK

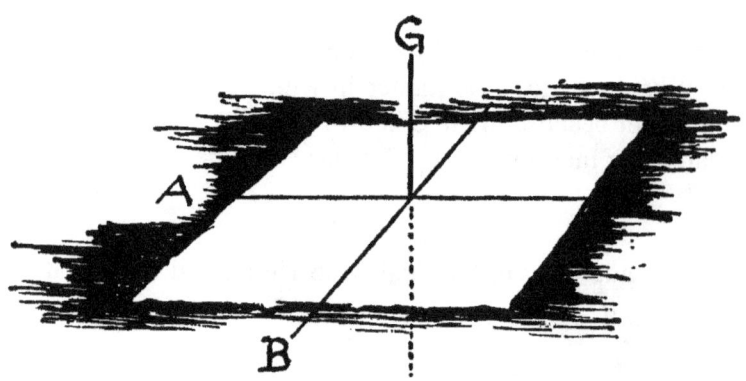

Human use of sun principles, on a planet, is in direct opposition to the creative principles of an, all wise God[11].

The law of reaction[32] will cancel every destructive cause. Apply sun principles on planets and the reaction will make the planet a sun[29]. Who escapes? Only the people who are with God[11] in the middle. How? They will be taken out into space by the race of Man in the spacecraft[18].

In order to present the one principle which causes all things to be, let us use the symbol "·G" to signify what is commonly referred to as God. Let us use "A" to symbolize the right hand of God[11], or the positive polarity, projective, male force of unbalanced energy. Let us use "B" as the sign of negative polarity, receptive, female energy, or the left hand of God.

Assume that God[11], who rested after the creation of all things, is the still fulcrum of Intelligence throughout all infinity that setves 'as the balance between these opposites.

CHAPTER ONE THE MISSING LINK

For an objective point of view, assume that the "G" line is vertical to the plane of the paper.

Assume that the "A" line is on the paper, running crosswise at 90° to the vertical "G" line. This "A" line of force is composed of positively charged particles.

Assume that the "B" line is running from the top to the botttom of the paper, at 90° to the "A" line and go·o to the "G" line. This "B" line of force is composed of negatively charged particles.

Where these lines cross there is an atom, a micro solar system, created in perfection by these unseen forces. The atomic element is determined by the substances present in the charged "A" and "B, lines. This evolves a nucleus of positively charged particles called a proton, surrounded by a field *of* negative orbits set up by the "B" particles in motion. The concentrated group of "B" particles in this orbit we call an electron.

The "G" line has no motion as to movement in a given direction. It extends infinitely throughout all space, through all substances and materials. It exists in what we term both light and darkness[30]. These lines are parallel to each other.

Atoms compose all things. "G" light is found in the composition of all atoms. "G" light is Creative intelligence. Our Earth[10]. is an electron of our Sun[29]., traveling in its orbit of a negative field. It is rotated by the band width of "A" and "B" light forces, equal to the Earth's[10]. diameter.

CHAPTER ONE THE MISSING LINK

Prior to the formation of individual atoms, the "A" and "B" lines of light force had to contain the correct amount of substance particles. For clarification let us revert down to a single line of "A" and "B" lines of force.

These two lines of oppositely charged light cross each other at 90°, insulated by the "G" lines of infinite Intelligence. They cannot be brought into induction where they cross unless they are mated.

In order to give birth to an atom of Hydrogen, the "A" and "B" lines *must* conform to species. The law reads "each after its own kind". The "B" must contain the same number of particles per inch as the "A" does. These particles must also vibrate at the same frequency.

In order to become Hydrogen both lines of light must conform to the vibratory frequency of Hydrogen in the spectrum. The vibratory frequency of each element is different. The Hydrogen particles vibrating in their own frequency in the light lines before they become an atom cannot mix with the frequency of any other element.

This makes them of like species in every respect except they are of opposite polarity. This opposition, of charge brings them together, and the "G" light allows them to mate by induction because they are equal opposites.

The density of each element is deterinined by the frequency of the vibrating particles in both the "A" and "B" lines of force.

Each atomic element is the result of perfect proportion, charge, and vibration in equal and opposite polarities. Thus an

CHAPTER ONE THE MISSING LINK

atom of Hydrogen is the same wherever it is found in the universe.

Let us proceed to simplify the complex Picture an onio cut in two. An onion is like an atom; the outside layer or shell being the negative field of orbit for the outertmost electron. The next layer and each alternate layer toward the center being composed of Intelligence, the insulating layer of infinite light force called the "G" line of light. Where you crack an atom, the force disturbing or, puncturing the outer shell creates unbalance and neutralizes the outer shell. This causes the outermost electron to be attracted to the positive proton in the center. However, before the electron reaches.The proton the instantaneous inrush of "G" light force through the fractured outer shell creates implosive pressures within the atom. This is the active Force that brings about the explosion when the electron and proton discharge within the ruptured shell. The insulating "G" light condenses into what science has named a neutrino. This potent causation force immediately deserts its wrecked atom and takes off to return to the thirteenth density. This is what religion would term a "resurrection[28]."; when the potent, causal, infinite, light force deserts its shell or body.

God[11] in His infinite Wisdom caused all of His creations to function by perpetual motion. He maintains the balance by centering each creation[16a] and insulating each one from all others.

When He created the "A" lines of light force, He caused to be 1850 of them to a square centimeter. He gave them positive polarity, male, projective gender, a speed of 186,000 miles per second, and matter in the form of charged particles.

CHAPTER ONE THE MISSING LINK

In opposition to the "A" lines of light force He created the "B" lines. The "B" lines are 125 7 per square centimeter. They cross between the "A" lines of force a 90° with a speed of 202,000 miles per second. Their polarity is <u>negative, their gender is female</u>[31], receptive.

Between the "breathing" of these two primary forces, He created rhythm. This brings about a "wave motion", which consolidates the individual lines into "bands". When "A" works inward, "B" works forward· and when "A" works outward ·"B" works backward. Rhythm, which establishes the "bands, levels, and density changes.", is operated by strain or desire. Strain is the time between the "flight" of the female, negative lines of force and "the pursuit" of the male, positive lines of force. When they encounter any created object that was "born" before by other "A" and "B" lines of light, they add to its rotation by spiral induction :and partial penetration.

The negative "B" lines are attracted to the Earth's[10]. positive core, but are resisted by the " G" light insulation strata. Having penetrated the negative crust, they are repelled by it and take the line of least resistance, which is out of the North Pole. By induction, they attracted the positive core To rotate in one direction, and in being repelled helped the negative crust to rotate in the opposite direction. The "A" positive lines of force work opposite to the foregoing, and are emitted at the ·South Pole. As they emit from the poles they are met by the "A" and "B" lines of light that are passing uninterrupted by the planet and bent back to their original course. The resistance in bending causes the aurora.

As they have reduced their energy charge and speed of motion in adding power to the planet, they enter different

CHAPTER ONE THE MISSING LINK

levels as they emerge from the poles. Then the "G" lines of light, crossing between them and insulating them, brings them back through "rest" and "rhythmic breathing" to their original conditions.

The "A" lines of force have more quantity "density" and less speed than the "B" lines of force. The "B" lines have more speed and less "density". This is the reason why the "A" positive lines of force charged with matter, become the proton core of the Earth[10]. The faster "B" charged matter becomes the crust of our planet. This strain or desire is the eternal progressive spirit in all things that manifest action.

Strain in people is called desire. When the desire exceeds the limits of capacity, the Father's agents of balance-the "A" or "B" lines of force will bring about an opposite result. The "G", "A", and , "B" lines are the ·"Us" referred to :irt the Bible (Gen.1: 26) when God[11]. said,· "Let *us* make man".

0 mortals,though My Laws have been as doormats beneath your feet; though through centuries you have· turned not to face the Light- I judge not,neither do I hold regrets, for all are given right to choose. Mortals in this density of three, having not chosen Me, now stand .beneath the whip, but are rather facing rebound of the actions man has created. My Laws are fixed. None can change the Law of all Infinity. One fulfills the Law, or faces judgment by the Law, written in the Light of each of My created beings. Having turned My Laws about, now you are faced with your man creations in opposition to My Law. So I gather up the scattered fruit, knowing that the bulk of My harvest has been lost to repetition upon repetition of errors, written in the history of mortals on this portion of Me. I must brush off this

CHAPTER ONE THE MISSING LINK

contamination from My cloak, that I may hang it in My closet clean. Those who have failed for centuries to recognize My person within their Being, are forced by their actiona to repetition once again.My heart, manifested by you, is Sore. But I shall recover to bring about the destiny as many times as necessary *that My pattern shall be complete for each one of My parts. So it is, again and again I cleanse My house. My love shall never fail. Everlasting* Light *is man's by* choice-alone, *and the choice I gave to him.*

I am the voice that manifest in every world you say. I am the sound in darkness to your ear, *that leads the way.*

You stumble on the path to Me. You fail to see the Light within that grows with every victory over self.

To be part of Me, project the actions of Me being you. Extend My Love instilled within. Do unto others as I do to you.

For I can only Be, through you.

CHAPTER TWO INVISIBLE GEARS

CHAPTER TWO

INVISIBLE GEARS

Densities are the levels or grades through which creation progresses. Thought is the image of the Creative Intelligence. Progression is a reward for effort expended in creative thought. Through thought the Creator[16] established a pattern through which all things must pass.

The first class passengers in this solar boat[40,39] are not the wealthy people, nor the intellectuals of the system. The steerage is not occupied by the poor or the illiterate. Everything in this boat is mixed up. The Creator[16] didn't make it this way, the mix-up is due to the doings of man.

Earth[10] people are dominated by individual and mass ego. Nearly everyone thinks he is better than others. Now progression is upward, and when one looks down on another he must lower himself to see the other. When one sees the good in others he automatically raises himself.

The Creator[16] established densities to control these conditions. The Third density[33], where these things exist in the triangle of confusion, is about all finished. Humans on Earth[10] are going to have to conform to the requirements of the Fourth density[34] or take this grade all over again.

The requirement to pass is to live the Golden Rule[35]. Not to profess it, or expect others to live it, but to live it individually,

CHAPTER TWO INVISIBLE GEARS

as you are only responsible for yourself.

The drawing represents one of the "flowers of the universe". The <u>Vela Sector System</u>[36] is only one of the Creator's[16] thoughts.

There are twelve densities in the system we occupy. Each of these is divided into twelve major cycles. Each major cycle is divided into twelve minor cycles. When a solar system moves out of one density into another, it is called a master cycle. The solar system that we are in is now in the arc between the Third and Fourth densities. For the planet Earth and this solar system, this is the time of times. The Earth[10] is culminating a minor cycle, a major cycle; and a master cycle all at the same time. This will bring about a <u>rebalancing of the planet on new poles</u>[37].When this occurs, the great earthquake written of in Revelations will take place.

The First density[38], for the Earth[10], was when the planet only supported vegetation. The Earth's[10] rotational speed was such that only gigantic vegetation with a germination temper.ature of around 110 degrees Fahrenheit could survive.

When the Earth[10] passed through the arc, or overlap between the First and Second densities, it rebalanced on new poles; and the massive vegetation became our coal beds of today.

As soon as the Earth[10] had stabilized in the Second density, the space people landed animals on the planet. This has been handed down from the ancient records as. the story of <u>Noah and the Ark</u>[39].

CHAPTER TWO INVISIBLE GEARS

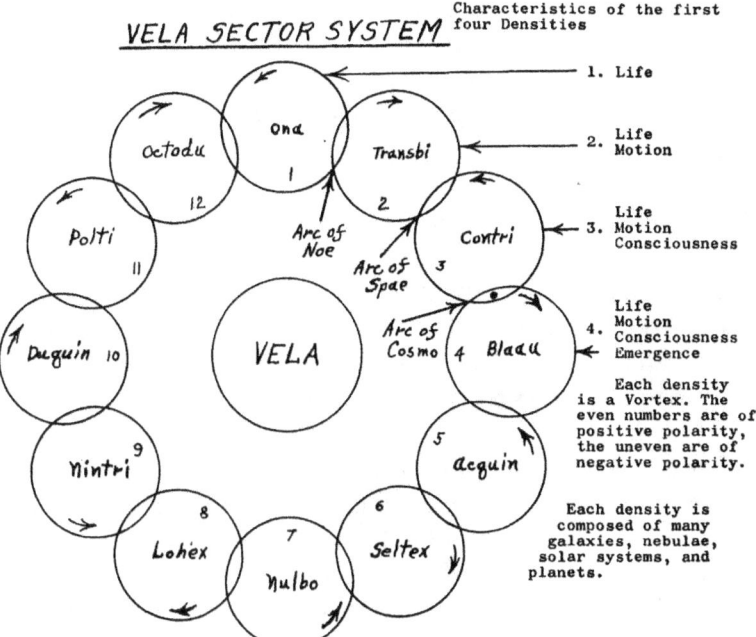

The Dot In The Arc Of Cosmo Depicts Our Solar System.

CHAPTER TWO INVISIBLE GEARS

The germination temperature in the Second density was 104 degrees. The animals that lived in the Second density were also large. They were of the mastodon and dinosaur types. The reason they became extinct when the planet passed from the Second into the Third density, was because the germination temperature in the Third density was around 98.6 degrees Fahrenheit.

Many of the carcasses of these large animals are recovered today from the glaciers of Siberia. That area was tropical in the Second density. In the arc of Spae, when the Earth[10] rebalanced on new poles, the animal with a germination temperature of 104 degrees Fahrenheit could not reproduce in a temperature of 98.6 degrees Fahrenheit.

After the large animals became extinct the space people of the Adamic Confederation landed a colony of the race of Man[15] on the Earth. It was through the mating of these Adamic Man people with the race of Eve[23] (upright-walking animals of high Second density development that survived the cataclysm in the arc of Spae) that brought about the humans of the Barth. This was the beginning of human people in the Third density, on the Earth[10]. The race of Eve[23] became extinct, except for the animal flesh contribution and destructive tendencies of humans.

Humans cannot reproduce in the Fourth density and will become extinct as an animal-Man mergence in the first 100 years, as the Fourth density germination temperature will be around 90 degrees Fahrenheit. The humans that survive through the cataclysm of the coming polar flip will gradually die off. The Fourth density is not for destructive principles or humans. Those who do not conform to the requirements to emerge will be reincarnated back into the 12th phase of the

CHAPTER TWO INVISIBLE GEARS

Third density on another planet, and have to live through this mess again.

The densities <u>alternate polarity</u>[37] and therefore rotation. The drawing shows them as viewed from the top, looking at their maximum circumference. An edgewise view would show them as spirals, one with the apex up and the next with the apex down. Our solar system is about to pass out of the maximum circumference of the Third density into the minimum circumference of the Fourth density. The Earth[10] will then rotate nearly 370 days in a year.

Do not confuse densities with dimensions. Densities are pressures established in changing frequencies of vibmtion. Dimensions are measurements. Some have mixed-up dimension and density. Time is not measurable in the Absolute. Time can be phased in density and moved backward or forward. However itt can only be done through the zero point between polarities.

As our solar system moves through space, its progression is into an ever increasing frequency of vibrations. Each solar system and every planet must evolve through grades, even as babies learn to crawl before they walk.

The "A" and "B" lines of force pass through your body at 90° to each other. The "G" line of infinite light centers your consciousness and separates you from all other people with a boundary of skin. As these positive and negative lines of energy pass through your body, they activate every atom and cell of your physical makeup.

If the approach of these lines to this planet, from out of space, is interrupted by one of the other planets, as they are, then

CHAPTER TWO INVISIBLE GEARS

you individually are affected by the influence from the other planets.

Our scientists say the Moon[50] causes tides, yet they contend that the Moon[50] has no effect on crops, people, or other conditions, that these beliefs are only superstition. The human body is over two-thirds water. Is it superstition to assume that if the influence of the Moon[50] moves thousands of millions of tons of water in the oceans, that the hundred pounds or so of water in a person is not also affected? Everything has some effect on everything else in the universe.

As you move throughout the day in an upright position, you are moving in and out of many lines of force. All of them are charged witth influences, not only of other planets but from other people, various metallic objects, electronic devices, and atmospheric conditions. You feel these influences and you may wonder how the day, or year, went so fast. At another time the hours may drag. These time changes are the results of some influence acting upon you.

If you work h1ard or run you become heated and tired. This is the result of an increase in the number of charged lines of force you have interrupted.

Through various attitudes caused by turning, bending, and motions of the limbs, heat is generated in the body because of constant changes of the "angle of attack" from the lines of force.

When you sit down to rest for a few minutes, this permits the body to absorb the energy from the "A" and "B" lines of force issuing forth from the same *unchanging* direction. Then the structure of the body cools off because it reaches balance.

CHAPTER TWO INVISIBLE GEARS

This idling condition of the body-motor is brought about by the fact that each atom is receiving steady motion by the same lines of force.

When you sleep at night the body becomes charged in balanced rhythmic interchange. There has been much said of one sleeping with the head to the North, or East, or in a particular direction. This is not a fixed law; it varies with each individual. Each person should try the various directions. With some people it would require that they vary direction occasionally.

It is more important to sleep away from metallic objec1ts. Coil springs are especially detrimental to complete rest. Metallic conductors set up vortices that cfause a circular motion within the straight lines of force. This is a parallelism to body activity; so instead of resting, your body is working even while you sleep.

The essence of life is the same in all densities or "dimensions". Life is manifested from the "A" and "B" lines of light force by the infinite "G" light. Life is only given form in the First density by the principle of "the wheel of life".

All vegetation, all substance with form such as rocks, fluids, and planets maintains form through various times, stages, or cycles.

Each form of life in the First density contributes substance to every other form of life on all material, or negative levels.

All densities of life contribute to the progression of every form of life in densities beneath them. All forms of substance are alive in repetitive patterns for their particular species.

CHAPTER TWO INVISIBLE GEARS

Thus substance, through life, repeats its cycles "from dust to dust".

Life is the carrier of progression in its eternal and endless spiral. Thus the stages are positive:

or negative balance:

or both:

when they are in balance.

The spiral[41] of life (also called Caduceus[42]) is symbolized by two serpents:

The negative, receptives or female:

CHAPTER TWO INVISIBLE GEARS

is only given desire by its opposite:

the positive, projective, or male counterpart and vice versa. These symbols are not zigzag in form, they are spiral. They are centered and separated by the "staff of life[43]":

around which they twine ever upward through the infinite Intelligence.

The First density on Earth[10], consisting mainly of vegetation, is of both polarities. The dividing line is the surface of the Earth[10]. The positive, projective part of the plant is attracted into the dark negative soil to provide minerals and moisture so the receptive, female portion above the surface may "bloom in her fullness".

This is the reason why a water-witcher's twig, taken from a living plant, can indicate water. It is actually a living

CHAPTER TWO INVISIBLE GEARS

instrument. Like magnets when they are cut, the positive end remains in thie same direction. Therefore they are held upside down in order to function. As all things beneath the surface of the soil are of negative polarity and since survival is the strongest desire, the twig wants to assume its natural polarity-position and is attracted, positive end butt first, to the "water of life". For the same reason, when you spend long periods of time in the positive sun, you require more water which is negative, to quench your thirst which is the result of unbalanced light force.

Every cell in the vegetation is life in form, maintaining a still greater life in form. As an animal eats the First density (stationary Life form) vegetation, It gives to It motion.

The substance confined to the place where the seed dropped can now move around, as it has been assimilated by and raised to the second density (Life and Motion).

The same progression of substance takes place when you eat the flesh of an animal. Humans being both animal and spirit, are of the Third density (Life, Motion and Consciousness).

You, as part of the eternal pattern of life in form, give to the animal substance the ability to express and recognize the spirit.

Although all forms of life progress within their own densities, much confusion has been started by the theorists who try to tie the densities together. Darwin tried to show the evolution of man from the apes. There is no missing link except breeding.

As our solar system has progressed through space it crossed

CHAPTER TWO INVISIBLE GEARS

on August 20, 1953, from the Third density to the Fourth density.

Our planet has emerged from the frequency of the Third density. Everything on this planet must now begin to conform to this higher frequency pattern.

We are on the verge of witnessing a cyclic, planetary housecleaning. All things in this solar system are going to be brought into balance.

The space people of the Adamic race, seirving as agents of God[11], have through the centuries followed a pattern of cycles in bringing their qualified teachers to the people of Earth[10].

Approximately every 2100 years the spacecraft[18] of the space people have landed one of their <u>Divine Mothers</u>[45] on Earth[10], to give birth to a "true son of God[11]". As £ar as the records go, they have all been "virgin mothers[10]".

These cycles are determined by the <u>Adamic people</u>[15] according to cosmic planetary time. A Minor Cycle is approximately 2,100 years, or one-twelfth of a Major Cycle.

A Major Cycle is about 26,000 years, or a complete cycle of the <u>Precession of the Equinox</u>[46]. These cycles vary in time either way, plus or minus, according to Nutation[44].

During the last Major Cycle the space people landed twelve teachers. The teacher called Jesus was the twelth and last of the "sons of God[11]" in the past Major Cycle.

The policy is always to retum the last teacher of each Major Cycle to begin the next cycle. The importance of today is

CHAPTER TWO INVISIBLE GEARS

emphasized by the fact that .we are not only on tthe pinnacle of a Minor Cycle, but are also amidst a Major, and Master Cycle at the same time. This brings about a balancing of the planetary forces that the space people call "the Father's[11] house cleaning among His planets". However, in the Bible it is called the time of the great earthquake[53].

Noah walked with God[11] because he was one of the space people who came to the Earth[10] in the "arc[39] of Noe".

In the Bible, Noah is confused with Noe. Noah was a man, and Noe was the "arc[39] of Noe".

It was in the "arc[39] of Noe" that the animals were brought to Earth[10]. The space people landed the various animals that could survive in the Second density germination temperature. Of course there was a flood[47] during the time of the "arc[39] of Noe". The Bible is correct when it. Said all the water[48] was in the firmament (in the First density). That was why the vegetation was so thick in the First density. The moisture would condense and water[48] the vegetation at night and rise as fog in the daytime.

When the Earth[10] flipped on its poles in the "arc[39] of Noe", the rotational speed changed and the new temperature of the Earth[10] being less, the waters[48] condensed and fell from the atmosphere and flooded[47] the land. The Bible says the waters[48] were fifteen cubits deep (about 27 feet) in Genesis, 7: 20.

So the story in the Bible of the ark[39] and its animal cargo, is a badly twisted version of a man and a boat[39]. The size of the Biblical ark[39] is given as 300 cubits long, 50 cubits wide and 30 cubits high, (about 525 feet, by 88 feet wide, by 53 feet

CHAPTER TWO INVISIBLE GEARS

high).

Imagine caging a pair of each kind of living thing in an area that large. And don't forget they needed sufficient food carried to feed them for 40[52] days.

Then the story gets further off. They confused the accurate, ancient records with another "arc". This was when the Bible story puts Noah's *sons*[51] in the same boat[39].

The animals were landed in the "arc[39] of Noe", between the First and Second densities. Three hundred and twelve thousand years later Ham, Shem, and Japheth[51] were landed on Earth[10] between the Second and Third densities, in the "arc[39] of Spae". Noah's "sons[51] " were not individuals either. The race of Ham[51] were the black people. The race of Shem[51] were white people, and the race of Japheth[51] were the yellow people.

The various tribes that descended from these three original colors of people, that were colonized on Earth[10] by the space people, is listed in Genesis, chapter 10.

Each race is pure in its own color. And the Universal law[49] reads "each seed after its own kind". In all the creations[16a] on the Earth[10], each flower, tree, animal and all of nature follows this Law[49] except humans who were given the right to choose. Humans were given the intelligence to raise themselves, yet humans are the only creatures that violate this Law[49].

> *0 man, though I am One, I am also Many.*
> *Though I center the individual light of each of you,*
> *you also are the One of Me. I live each sensation;*
> *I live every expression; I am the motion of thee,*

CHAPTER TWO INVISIBLE GEARS

*0 man. Consider each thing you do, you do to Me.
For when you strike one of My parts I feel the blow.
And when you cast a thought of love, I absorb the
love of you; and I return it too. When idle mind
leads thee to tear the reputation of another down,
you have only lowered your thought of Me, and in
turn have lowered yourself. Realize that I am always
with you. Always the silent, unseen, companion to
your every action; the recipient of your every
thought. I love to express Myself through you in
ways that bring Me joy; in paths that reach the
hearts in gratitude. Help Me to express the Oneness
of each of Us that I may center all My parts
in unity of Me and thee in harmony and Love; that
none shall know the pain, and sorrow, and heartbreak
you did express yourself. I gave thee Light
of Life that you might extend My action; that others
might feel the Joy of Me that are in darkness bent,
who are trouble-blinded and cannot see that I am
there. Extend the progress I have brought into being
by lifting up another, that I may feel the twofold
expression expressed in grateful thanks.*

*Though I am stillness, My parts all move in Me.
My rest is in contrast, or motion could not be. Extremes
establish the boundaries beyond which man
cannot go. Though I am boundless, man is bound
in Being of Me, by individuality.*

*Man I have created so I may extend Myself
through motion of the parts of Me, so I will not be
bound within the stillness of My infinity.*

CHAPTER THREE SUN OF GOD

CHAPTER THREE

SUN[29] OF GODS[11]

The Sun[29] is an evolved planet in its progressive state of becoming space. An expanding universe must have something to expand from. The Sun is not becoming smaller by combustion, fission or fusion. It is growing larger by digestion of the matter it encounters in the lines of primary light energy. The Sun[11] gives off only a very small percentage of the energy it is thus acquiring. Matter, or mass, cannot give off but only a small percentage of its actual total potential energy, even in the famed atomic bombs.

The energy given off by any fuel or matter is always less than that substance which went into its making. Why is this?

The answer is because *Mind* also went into the making of all created things. Mind[5] is neutral. Mind cannot give off energy, it can only direct the flow and action of energy. Universal Mind[4] permeates all things. Each person uses the Mind[5] of God[11] according to his, or her ability to get into It deeper. All things that are, or ever will be, already exist in Universal Mind[4]. None can penetrate into the Universal Mind[4] beyond their own acquired capability. On the other hand, God[11] cannot do more for you than you are capable of doing for yourself by directing the Universal Mind[4].

CHAPTER THREE SUN OF GOD

When scientists discovers that the core of the proton in an atom is square, then they will realize that the body in the Sun[29] is also square.

The cubic minerals in their crystallized state are of neutral polarity on a negative surface such as the Earth[10]. They can be brought into polarity however, by exposure to light, pressure, or charging.

The body of the Sun[29] was brought into cubic form by the fact that its axes were parallel to the three lines of light energy. The <u>infinite light (Universal Mind[4])</u> , or the "G" line of light centers one axis. The positive "A" and the negative "B" lines center the other two axes. They are all at 90° angles to each other.

The sunspots are discharges of secondary magnetic (electrostatic) force released into the actisphere and photosphere by the rotating corners of the square core body. These discharges are magnetic exhaust effects common to any body in motion.

The sunspots are apparent in the 10° to 30° North and South latitudes on the Sun[29], to our vision. The sunspots are exhausted when the discharged polarized matter is neutralized in the photosphere or the actisphere. They appear black to Barth telescopes, because they hide the effect of fusion taking place between the positive photosphere and the negative actisphere.

The positive photosphere to the positive Sun[29] body is the

CHAPTER THREE SUN OF GOD

equivalent of the negative atmosphere to the negative Earth[10] body they each carry the same polarity as the body which they surround.

The act that the rotational period of the Sun[29] appears to be of different speeds at different latitudes, is due to the spiral[41] effects of primary light energy losing speed in its travel to the poles. The apparent ten day differential in rotation between the equator of the Sun[29] and its poles is only obsetved in the force field of the actisphere.

Viewed from the point of any of the three axes, a cube will appear square around its perimeter. Many square, positive bodies in space do not rotate, because their axes remain parallel to the lines of primary light.

The bodies that do rotate were placed in motion when their axes were thrown out of parallel with the lines of light, by a bend, or warp in the lines of primary energy. This caused the positive, square body 'to start rotating by unbalanced polarity opposition within itself. The polar axis of the Sun[29] is now through two opposite comers of the cubic sun[29] body. The cube remained motionless in the lines of primary energy, like a compass needle, as long as it was in polarity balance.

Once the body was in motion, the lines of force, trying to reach rest, spiraled to tthe two points of least motion. This established an equator and opposite poles at two opposite corners.

CHAPTER THREE SUN OF GOD

The Sun – Governor of our Solar System

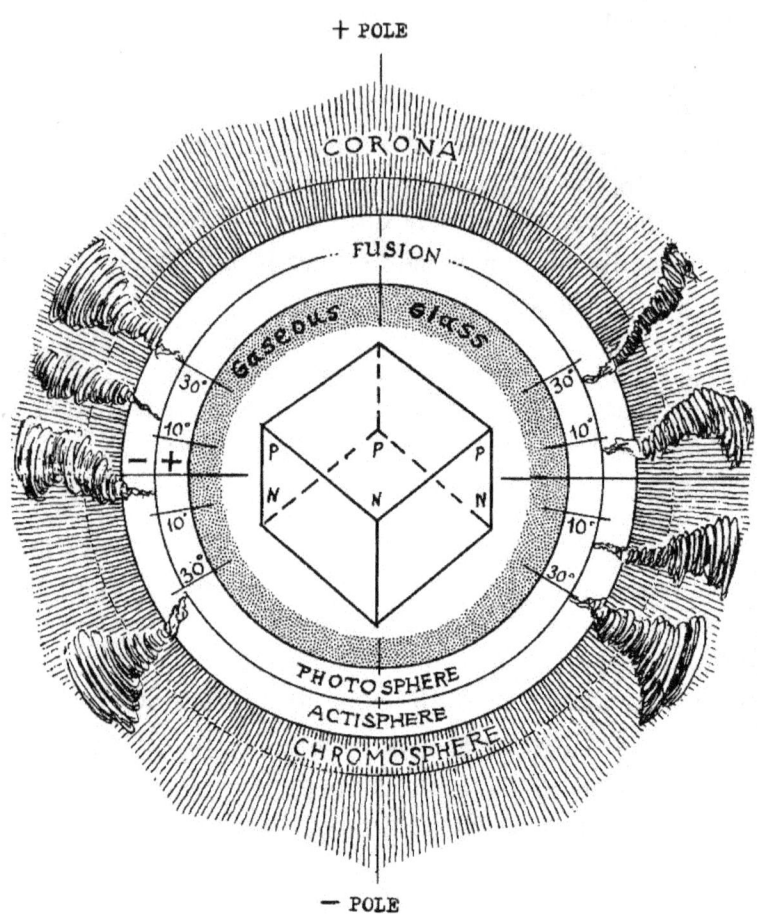

CHAPTER THREE SUN OF GOD

In this position the positive polarity half, and the negative polarity half of the Sun[29], each has three comers discharging at approximately 20° each side of the equator. These rotating corners are displacing matter and discharging energy; this is what causes the sunspots.

Cut an artgum eraser, or a piece of soap, into a cube and insert common pins in two opposite corners. Then make a line around the cube midway between the pole points, or pins. Assume one half of the cube will have four[52] comers in it of one polarity. Then if you look at the opposite comers you will find they are all on the other side of the equator line.

You will also see that each half, from the equator line, is a three sided pyramid, or prism. The polarized prismic structure of the rotating Sun[29] generates secondary light in its positive photosphere. The negative actisphere, which we see as a ball of fire, is activated in opposition tto the photosphere by the primary lines of light energy.

Space is the cubes of matter that are stable, because their three axes are parallel to the three lines of light. Motion is only manifested by unbalanced matter; whether it be a sun, planet, atom, or person.

Desire for rest is what causes the Intelligence in matter in motion to seek balance and become again part of the infinite Intelligence, which is still. Space is composed of balanced cubes of Intelligence at rest.

The lines of primary light energy parallel the eight[54] edges

CHAPTER THREE SUN OF GOD

and two axes of the cubes of space in two directions, and the infinite light parallels the four remaining edges and one axis.

All unbalanced, positive bodies are emitting light. All unbalanced, negative bodies are absorbing light. Cubes are unbal.anced, positive bodies. Negative bodies are unbalanced spheres. Each can contain, or be a part of the other; as long as one polarity is predominant. The predominant polarity will determine whether the object is spherical or cubical in shape.

Astronomers state that the light from some of the stars is coming from so many hundreds and thousands of light years away, that the star could be burned outt and the light would still be visible on the Earth[10]. This is predicated on the idea that the light is still traveling after the emitting body is no longer there. This is erroneous. If the stars were not still emitting light, and were not there, you could not see it.

Telescopes and eyes do not see! They are only a system of lenses through which light passes. The mind sees. You can picture things you have experienced in the mind with your eyes closed.

The same infinite light of Intelligent Mind[5] centers every atom, star, planet, and manifested being. When astronomers look through a telescope, or people obsetve without one; anything you can see is there. The instant, infinite, light of Universal Mind[4] that centers you and what your mind sees; cannot record, or vision something that is not there.

Negative, physical vision only records to the negative, physical brain the illusion that the Sun[29] is round. All that the

CHAPTER THREE SUN OF GOD

limited physical vision is recording is the effect of the secondary light emissions from the force field in fusion around the Sun[29].

Physical, negative vision can only see reflected, positive light from another negative body; or negative light reflected from ! another positive body. The actisphere being of negative polarity, is spherical. Therefore, the negative, physical vision records it as a ball of fire. Were it not for the activation of the Sun's[29] actisphere by the positive and negative lines of primary light energy, you would not see the Sun[29] at all with physical vision.

Though I scatter My seeds of Light throughout My garden of space, I determine which shall grow to be a star and which shall represent My Image.

Though all My seeds are Light of Me, each brings about a pattern individual in destiny of My doing.

Though in the scattering of My seeds some may fall on barren soil, the segregation is within the knowing which shall bear fruit. For in the essence of My Wisdom I breathe not the breath of Life that all My seeds shall grow at once. Rather do I select them that I may express Myself each moment throughout eternal time. And though my seeds are pure in Light and Love of Me, I know all shall not grow to bring about the fruit in perfection. For unto each seed I rendered individuality and right to choose.

0 man, 0 mortal man, My Oneness I bring about in individuality that I may scatter My parts and express Myself. Though all things I have created in balanced opposites, I

CHAPTER THREE SUN OF GOD

remain the centering separator. Though I have made My gender two, though My polarity is divided, I test My strength on My right and My left. Though man has chosen to further separate My expressions of Love; though man has chosen to divide the roads to Me; though man has brought self-interest into My expression I still maintain the balance, centering My interchange of powers. If one should sit on My right hand in the Love of Me, I shaJl balance that Love upon My left hand in equality. I cast out barriers to face the Beings of you, that I may temper all My parts. Though I have given all alike from thought of Me, *many cannot reach the door that guides their destiny to paths unfurled in Light. And though they lose their way in darkness seeking retrieve the whole and cast My mold again, never losing any* single *portion. For I a in Soul of thee, 0 man, and Light and Darkness too. An tough my Light of right extends through all eternity, I back the- Light with -Darkness, that recognition may be yours.*

Energy and matter are opposite poles of the same thing. Matter can be converted into energy, but always with mass loss. Energy; in being converted to matter, will always register a gain. The fact that all celestial bodies are conversions to matter of energy in solultion in space, is evidenced by their different densities. Scientists have assumed that if a rocket could

The "time" field of the Sun[29] establishes a zero field of time relative to the planet's opposition of hemispherical polarities. The opposition of the Earth's[11] polarities relative to the energy charge of its mass is what establishes its position in the solar system.

A small planet can be of greater density than a larger one. Its

CHAPTER THREE SUN OF GOD

composition of the elements may be such, however, that its charge relative to its mass may be less.

The "time" field of the Earth[10] is at the magnetic equator. At the Earth's[10] surface it is narrowed down to about the thickness of a razor blade.

Surface land is of greater magnetic potential than the oceans. The Earth's[10] magnetic equator therefore will be inclined to veer toward the major land masses. This wave in the magnettic equator stabilizes as it recedes from the surface.

The angle of divergence is about 5° of arc, making a "V"-shaped cross section as it gains altitude from the Surface.

The area composing this "V"-shaped cross section is the Earth's[10] "time" field.

If you could stay in this area a few thousand miles from the Earth's[10] surface, time would cease to exist. Your body polarities would reach balance, and you would become pure Mind[5] and infinite in your scope of everything.

It is the "time" field that separates polarities in their different speeds of apparent rotation.

Relative to the Earth[10], the positive and negative lines of primary energy are working in opposition. The negative lines of force are causing the Earth[10] to rotate, while the positive lines of force are trying to stop it from rotating. The speed of the Earth's[10] rotation is the result of the differential between

CHAPTER THREE SUN OF GOD

the speed of the positive lines of force and the speed of the negative lines of force, relative to the charge of the Earth's[10] mass.

The positive and negative lines of force fill space with matter in solution. Being in solution, it must be tertned energy, because it is not condensed by polarity predominance.

The "time" field ends at the outter limit of the Earth's[10] force field. If it were possible to alter the "time" field by changing it relative to the Earth's[10] magnetic equator, we could direct the planet's course out of the solar system, or cause it to assume another orbit elsewhere in the system.

The spacecraft are controlled in their travel by oscillating the "time" field with thought force, causing the positive and negative fields to move the ship's mass relative to the direction of the lines of primary energy.

Earth[10] scientists do not understand negative electrical currents, or fields. As the positive lines of force manifest results through conductors, the negative currents and fields can only be activated through non-conductors. The only true insulation that will separate the opposite polarities of fields is time. The Earth's[10] people only register time because the planet rotates and orbits. They assume that "time goes by". Time is infinite, and all that people on a planet can register is the revolving planet passing through time. The people are in motion on the planet, so they assume that time is in motion. Actually they lare moving through time with no visible means of registering the illness of time. If time ever moves it will cause everything in the universe to collide, and all

CHAPTER THREE SUN OF GOD

condensed energy, or matter, would go back into solution in space.

When the scientists try to push a rocket through space by brute force, instead of going with the currents of primary energy carrying matter in solution in space, they will discover that matter in solution (energy) or space is anything but void.

The speed of light, established at 186,000 miles per second, is *not* its speed. IIt is the speed of the positive "A" lines of force that extend throughout space. The speed of the negative "B" lines of force, at 90° to the positive lines, is 202,000 miles per second. The speed of magnetism is the combined speeds of the positive and negative lines of force, or 388,000 miles per second. The difference between the positive and negative lines of force is 16,000 miles per second.

The spacecraft[18] use this differential to cycle or phase their power. This accounts for their appearance of skipping. Their ships are caused to attract or repel the lines of force which are at right angles to their diredtion of travel.

The spacecraft[18] can move through our dense, lower atmosphere at many thousands of miles per hour, because they bring their own "space" with them. The force field around each ship[18,39] does not allow our air to enter the field, consequently the ship[18,39] dees not get hot by friction. The ship[18,39], inside of its own force field, is protected by the field from debris in space, from air in density, and from sound shock waves. As no sound can penetrate through the field, they travel silently through our skies; except at very slow speeds or when hovering, they transmit a humming, throbbing

CHAPTER THREE SUN OF GOD

tone. The field increases its resistance and strength when the speed of the ship[18,39] increases.

Space is infiltrated with debris. No principle of rocket propelled missiles or ships is practicable outside of our Earth's[10] force field, as rockets do not create a protective field around themselves. Some of the debris, from the size of grains of rice to rocks larger than buildings, are traveling at speeds of hundreds of miles per second.

Our planet operates in a self-generated magnetic field. Meteorites do not bum out in our atmosphere because they encounter oxygen. They disintegrate in the Earth's[10]. protective field of force. If the meteorite is negatively charged it disintegrates in, the positively charged s trata of the force field.

Our spacecraft[18] the Barth, operates in a field vortex of the Sun[29]. The Earth[10] is a combination battery, generator, and motor. Our atmosphere serves as a brush, a field, and a bearing. Our heat comes from our dense, surface atmosphere. The only reason we feel more heat on the side toward the Sun[29] is because the positive Sun causes a "brush effect" in our negative, surface atmosphere. The crust commutator is warmed from resistance and friction; while both rotating the planet as a motor, and generating the force field.

Gravity is not attraction, nor "magnetism". Gravity is "resistance pressure" brought about in all objects, bodies, or substances by the lines of force penetrating tthem toward the center of the Earth[10.]

CHAPTER THREE SUN OF GOD

The "A" positive (male) projective lines of force are trying to reach discharge, or impregnation in the negative (female) crust.

The "B" negative (female) receptive lines of force are trying to reach fecundation or productive powers from .the positive male core.

The two lines of force "A" and "B" are working together, in opposition, to supply power for the continuous functions on and in the sphere and atmosphere, while the Father[11,16] centers the balanced control through the "G" lines of light.

Since the negative lines of force move faster than the positive lines, a negative body will always rotate counterclockwise from one viewpoint, and a positively charged body will rotate clockwise from the same viewpoint.

The measurable speed of positive or negative lines of light energy will vary with the orbit of any planet. Measurements of light energy of positive polarity will conform to the orbit diameter of any given planet. Measurements of negative polarity light energy will exceed the orbit diameter. Negative light energy cannot be accurately measured from the surface of a negatively charged planet, such as the Earth.

When the atmosphere of negative nature, such as the Earth's, is balanced by positive charges from fusion particles, it will cause moisture in the atmosphere to pile up at one magnetic pole and recede from the opposite polarity pole. It will cause a change in the planet's rotation speed; and due to germination temperature change, the eventual extinction of

CHAPTER THREE SUN OF GOD

life forms that conform to that germination temperature. An excess of positively charged particles in the negative atmosphere will cause a planet to seek balance on new poles.

Positive and negative lines of light force are always in an unbalanced state due to their different speeds of travel. When they are interrupted by a body or planet, they bring about motion because of their differential, or the desire to reach rest. If the Earth's[10] poles were vertical instead of inclined, the Earth's[10] orbit[46] would be round instead of elliptical[46]. If there were as much land south of the Equator as there is north of it, the Earth's[10] axis[46] would not be inclined.

Magnetism is not the causal force, but is the result or exhaust effect of light forces of positive and negative polarity in action. A magnet **is** not *charged* with magnetism. It is only serving as a polarity conductor of the lines of light energy passing through it. Both poles will *attract* a non-polarized conductor. Either pole will attract its opposite polarity or repel a like polarity.

Influences of a negative nature lead tthe minds of humans to try to bring about positive effects. When these positive effects exceed the balance of natural negative charges on a negative planet, then the planet will rebalance itself to conform to the light lines of force.

Man is mostly space, filled with substance in form. The body does not derive energy from the food assimilated by it. The food is only transformed to become a conductor for light energy passing through the body.

Power is only manifested through motion. Controlled power

CHAPTER THREE SUN OF GOD

is that which is given direction. The discovery of the wheel gave mankind the means to an endless track of motion.

Universal[4] power throughout infinite space is demonstrated in the guided motion of all planets, moons, suns, galaxies, and nebulae. None of these are haphazardly flying through space uncontrolled. Their course, orbit, rotation, and separation are maintained by precision interchange of reltative power. All bodies in space are motored by primary light energy. Solar emanations and atomic energy are secondary powers or effects of the primary light energy in motion.

The cross, in one shape or another, has always been the symbol of spiritual power. Scientifically, spiritual power is unseen power. Spiritual power can only be understood when it is manifest in the seen effect. This seen effect may be either in the range of the physical vision or outside of the physical limits.

Primary light energy functions in many unlimited conditions and frequencies above and below the limits of physical vision. Everything in space that rotates, orbits, or manifests motion as to direction, is powered by primary light energy. Wherever a body interrupts the lines of primary light, motion is effected. This is an immutable law.

Within the human body is a universe in miniature. The axis of every crystal, atom, planet, or person is centered in unseen light of unlimited extent. The manifested boundaries or surface of any of these are insulated from all others of like polarity.The eternal existence of all of these is encompassed within the center of the axis.

CHAPTER THREE SUN OF GOD

The cross[52] is the symbol of power of the opposite polarities. By interrupting the primary lines of positive and negative light energy, a differential is established. By phasing this differential, controlled power is established in motion. This is the long hidden secret of the Maltese cross[55] "Mal" means negative tongues of flame, or static electricity; "tese" means interchange, two-in-one or differential between. When the differential between the positive and negative forces of light energy are controlled by phasing they result in unlimited power through motion. If the motion exceeds the differential phase, disintegration will result.

Electricity is a by-product of magnetism. Gravity is the resistance pressure set up by the opposition of differential between the causal light energy and the effect-magnetism.

Though I have set the patterns of My doing all about you, yet you see them not. I scatter seeds of Light, I cast the shadows man calls day, and shadows of the shadows man calls night_, in repetition. I have paved the way for man to see. Has not My pattern stood the test to build another bird a nest again, where others were before? Cannot you see, 0 man of Me do as I say, do as I do. Do as I cause the way to be, within your understanding of the Me in thee. Look to the pattern all around; the fragrance of the essence of My Love in flowers you have found; and in the cool, beneath the tree, there I am to comfort you and yet you question parts of Me. Throughout My Being, I made thee man to carry on, to take the stand in My defense; to build the wall, to scale the fence of destiny. Not to follow whims of chance along the side; not to fall beneath

CHAPTER THREE SUN OF GOD

the wheels of hate and fear, that others may ride in comfort. Only look, feel the essence of My Being. Absorb Me in the breeze. Reach Me in the sun. My heart is warm, you are the one. Never have I set a pattern to lead you all astray. Any fear you feel, 0 man, you make along the way to Me and your arrival is delayed. Your stage is set, the curtain must come down, but only to go up again. My pattern is eternity. Repetition is the grade that leads to Me, 0 man.

From the harvest of My golden grain I separate the chaff. I break the bonds of freedom, lest man shall undo My works. I bring about a change in cycles so My balance shall not be disturbed.

For when My Laws are superseded, then must I strike from out the night and scourge contamination from My Being.

For I am Love, and I am freedom unto all My parts, but no part shall bind Me to destruction. So as in times gone past; I wreak My wrath, I cleanse My house, I upset My creations for none shall be above Me!

CHAPTER FOUR TRINITY OF INFINITY

CHAPTER FOUR

TRINITY[56] OF INFINITY[57]

Time is only understood by each conscious, intelligent unit from its established point of location motion.

Time cannot be measured, only the repetition of motions manifested as beginnings and endings can be measured.

Each point of beginning and ending is only relative to the understanding of the individual establishing his point of view

The point of begin and end is established by one individual, so as to bring another individual to the same point of understanding.

Life, time and Being[58] are understandable to Intelligence alone. These three are non-existent only when Intelligence has been excluded by ignorance in the individual.

Life, time and Being[58] can only exist in space, which is also infinite.

Space is solution, composed of Life, time, Being[58], and Inteligence. None of these can be measured in the Absolute. They can only enter measurable dimension when individuals establish points from which to measure.

Length, height, and width; these are only three measurements

CHAPTER FOUR TRINITY OF INFINITY

by which individuals can understand points from which relative measurements are started and ended.

An inch, a foot, or a yard, are not understood by people who use some other devised means of measurement. A relative difference between the measure. ments must be charted in order to understand the difference between their system and ours.

Measurements can only be achieved in and by motions. No day or night could be measured without the motion of the Earth[10] revolving. No seasons or years would exist if the Earth[51] didn't orbit around the Sun[29].

The life span of people on the Earth[10] is only arrived at by the measurement of people's time on Earth[10] relative to past measurements. Belief (the illusion of reality) makes people accept the established record of the life spans of other people who have lived before them, as a measure by which they should live and then die.

The establishment of these points of beginning and end of life are only manifest in matter which has little or no Intelligence.

Matter cannot manifest motion without energy. Energy is the motion of thought manifested through matter. Intelligence which has no motion can only manifest through thought, which causes motion to be manifest in matter by thought force.

CHAPTER FOUR TRINITY OF INFINITY

In symbology the Creator[16] is expressed by:

This signifies the circumference[59] encompassing every thing. The circle is an endless line signifying infinity with no beginning and no end.

Life is an essence of the infinite solution we call space. You are living in an endless ocean of life, as are the atoms, planets, and suns. You could not manifest life, if life were not where you are. Since life manifests everywhere in infinity, you cannot end life, or begin life. You cari only establish a point in the endless circle[59]:

where you began the cycle[59] of manifesting matter in life.

Motion can be symbolized in the endless circle[59] by the sign of an arrow:

An arrow has always signified "the way to go". All matter manifesting life in balanced motion moves in an arc. All matter manifesting life in unbalance, or un-natural principles, is symbolized by an angle:

The largest portion of you is space, whether it be the space in atoms, cells, or tissue composing the matter of your physical body; or the space your limited body as a unit occupies.

CHAPTER FOUR TRINITY OF INFINITY

Your intelligence is established by the limits of your individual concepts. Everyone uses the One[9] Mind. Your limit is only a measurement of your ability to penetrate and absorb to the full your capacity of the infinite Intelligence. Time is variable in your concept of it. *One*[9] day seems longer, or shorter, than another day.

You are an assembly of other forms of individual manifested life. You are a form enclosing various compositions of atomic, molecular, crystalline, and cellular structure. In turn you are a small individual part of a living planet, solar system, and galaxy.

Change is the result of motion. Time is measurable only in cycles of repetition.

Every thought sets up motion. Every motion causes an effect. Your manifestation of matter in motion is the reflection of your true concept, and understanding, of Infinity.

Things in motion change, and things that change are not eternal in any one pattern of form.

"T" is the symbol of time.
"S" is the symbol of space.
"B" is the symbol of Being[58].

is the Caduceus[42], or the triune of "T",

CHAPTER FOUR TRINITY OF INFINITY

"B", and "S". Division of the eternal things is what created opposites[30].

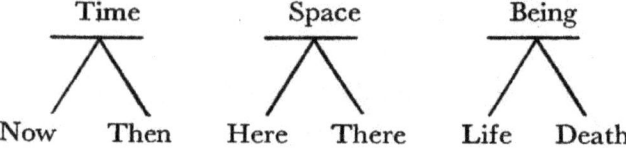

Cycles[59] are repetitions of the divisions. All divisions of opposites[30] reach a fulcrum pinnacle of stillness, at times. Everything in the universe comes under one; or. the other, of the three aspects of infinity[57].

Each of the opposites[30], such as here and there, cycles[59] an interchange within itself like a swinging pendulum. "Here" becomes "there" as soon as you cross the street, and "there" becomes "here". As you register your own changes in time, "'tomorrow" becomes "today" as the Earth[10] revolves on its axis, and "today" was "tomorrow" yesterday.

Life and death also interchange, so that Being[58] may manifest through the action.

Time cannot be a dimension, because everything in motion in time will never repeat itself again exactly as it was before.

If you could be *not,* then you could not be *now,* because now

CHAPTER FOUR TRINITY OF INFINITY

was then before you arrived here from there. You *are* all the time, even when your body sleeps. The real You never sleeps, although it rests at the peak of the fulcrum in the interchange between the opposites[30] of life and death.

Flesh is only matter you assimilate as a requirement of this dense Earthly condition. Flesh moves only because your real body moves it. Your matter body of flesh is not going to walk, or talk, after you get out of it. *Death* can only manifest in matter. This is the interchange that permits matter to return to what it was before you assimilated it into form.

That portion of space which is *You,* will always *Be* in *time* somewhere. Expressing *life here now* is really *death there then,* when you observe from the opposite side of things.

The trinity[56] of time, space, and Being are the deity called ,God[11].

Time, like thought, is infinite. Time does not "go by". Everything that moves in the universe goes *through* time. Man measures time with clocks and calendars. If there were no measuring methods made by man, then there would be no yesteryears or tomorrows. Age would not exist, today would be all there is.

Individual beings are all part of each other in the universal sense, making up Infinite Being[58]. God[11] is not an individual, but is all of us. God[11] being infinite and boundless, He is not something or someone man finds on the other side of the door called death. If this were true, He would not be infinite[12].

CHAPTER FOUR TRINITY OF INFINITY

Time is a medium through which the beings of God's[11] creation[16a] manifest God's[11] Presence. No one can live in the past or the future who is not present now in God[11].

Mind through thought is not limited to the present, for thought is also infinite. The Creative Mind of today is the same infinite Mind that created the universe. Mind is God[11] manifested in Be-ing[58]. Your part of God is manifested when you use God's[11] infinite Mind to create through thought. Thought is the creative force that gives Life to Be-ing[58].

Space is not void. Space is the essence of Intelligent Mind. Man is a space filled with creative matter, manifesting the thought essence of form. And so are all things with life.

Man is in God's[11] Image only when the thought of infinite Mind is brought into being by individual thought to manifest other creative forms in time.

Objects, structures, and things cannot manifest creative thought; as they do not move through infinite time as individual parts of space, or the essence of Intelligence.

To be, man must manifest motion in the medium of time, which stands still. Anyone who does not "have time" to manifest God's[11] doing, has discarded thought and life. The matter manifesting their form will soon become inert. Death is not "a doorway to God in heaven". Heaven is a doorway to God[11] on Earth[10].

CHAPTER FOUR TRINITY OF INFINITY

Mortals bound in density who would be the cause, who would bide my time, the tree of thee in Me stops not its growth, Though My parts would add to My divisions, My faceless cosmic clock records no time. For man is not a cause, but rather a result of Me, for I alone am cause of things to be. And though thou mortal man would wind My clock of destiny, and set the powder keg of destruction at My feet, how can he know the woe? For I alone am cause and man is the result of Me, bound to destiny. And in destruction-bent reverses course and all the Light spent in his Being is hidden by the curtain of ignorance drawn before Me. Though I alone am cause, My wrath is not aroused. I tear the shroud. I bring man back through birth within the Light, and test My right expressed in progression of My parts. I write the drama, man plays the fool, then I applaud and make the tool sharper to My cause through experienced results. Man cannot set My clock, for I alone can read the time of My eternity. And so it is I set the stage, I play the parts, I cause the curtain to come down while man sits in the audience of My universe applauding, not knowing why.

Though I have scattered My creations throughout the endless space of Me, I use My tools to manifest My doings. To do My works no task is small. I choose My tools, I trust them all until they fail Me. Then I put another to the test.

My tools are not the tools of man, that rust and break and fall away. My tools are living instruments that work with love throughout the day and night. To each I gave the choice to be an instrument of Me.

CHAPTER FIVE   UNSEEN SCALES

CHAPTER FIVE

UNSEEN SCALES

The accompanying drawing is to explain the one universal principle of Life. This principle is standard on any planet in space, and in all life forms, whether insect, animal, bird, human, Man or spirit.

In the drawing you are looking at the cut ends of the negative "B" lines of light energy of course greatly enlarged. They are traveling away from you and rotating in a counter-clockwise direction. These are the female, receptive, negative polarity lines of light energy.

At right angles, or 90° to the "B" lines of light energy are the positive "A" lines, traveling from left to right and rotating in a clockwise direction.

These two lines of light energy can only unite in birth or death. Birth by induction, and death by shortcircuiting.

God[11] controls physical birth and death by allowing the rebirth of individuals through the living instruments of His choosing. Only when He[16] removes His insulating qualities can a seen be born into another repetition of life progression.

Only when you have lived His[16] purpose for you, in each life grade, does He graduate you into the next grade.

CHAPTER FIVE   UNSEEN SCALES

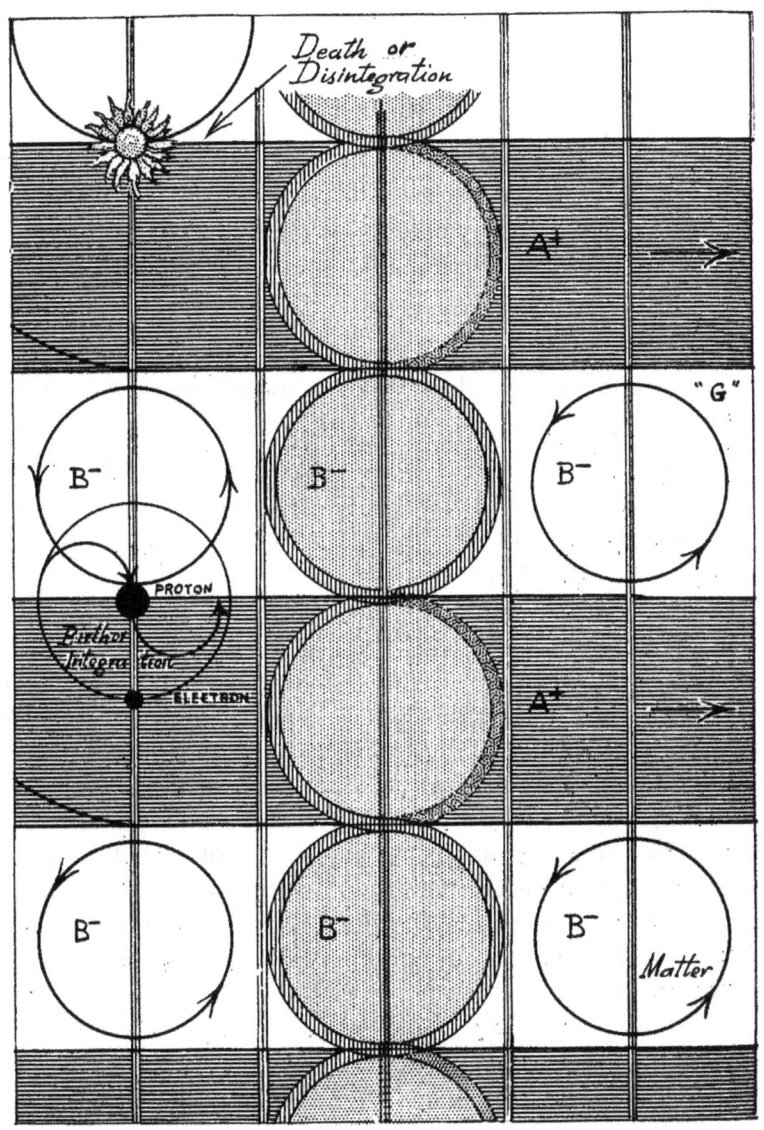

CHAPTER FIVE   UNSEEN SCALES

If your actions prove to Him[16] that through violation of His infinite laws[60] you will not pass this grade

then you die physically and your eternal, atomic cluster of consciousness is brought back through rebirth into the same grade in order to pass on to the next higher grade. Rebirth into the same grade, because of failure to pass it, is the only time that the so-called "reincarnation[14]" takes place.

When you were created as Man in God's[11] Image, you were made an atom of matter, charged with opposite polarities in your proton-electron individuality. You were given individual motion. The space within your electron orbit shell boundary was endowed by the Creative Spirit with His unseen Intelligence.

As you progressed through the mobile highways of lighlt energy, you encountered the experience of meeting other atoms· of different elements of matter. With each new experience you added another atom to your consciousness. Soon the consciousness began to increase in size, composed of many atoms of different experiences and of different elements. Your consciousness is composed of the same number of atoms as the number of experiences you have had since your creation as an individual. Experience is recorded in the consciousness. And in consciousness is the eternal record of your knowing.

Education and learning are recorded in the brain and can only be used in this *mortal* grade of life. When the brain is buried with the body all the learning and intellectual education

CHAPTER FIVE UNSEEN SCALES

ends; unless it has been applied through experience.

To reach the true Intelligence of your many experiences and permanent knowledge requires going within; through meditation you can become aware of your consciousness and unseen Intelligence you accumulated in the past.

The largest portion of your original atom creation was the space within the shell boundary. This space is, was, and will always be the unseen portion of your part of the Supreme Intelligence.

As you travel through, the maze of life lines you often encounter resistance, set up by those who think they are going in the right direction and that you should conform to their direction of travel. But each was given the individual right to choose his direction. Scientifically the correct course is at 45° to the lines of light, and in a progressive spiral into finer frequencies of light. This maintains the balance between the positive and negative[30] lines of light energy.

Every body that interrupts the lines of force will establish a "field" around itself.

Stationary bodies such as trees, rocks, or mountains, establish "fields" the same as atoms, planets, or suns[29]. On a surface of negative polarity the *height* of every species is stablished by the "field" around it; therefore vegetation and trees grow to a common species average.

The "field" set up in a tree is such that the lines of force passing through the tree establish a vortex in its body. This vortex starts at the surface of the ground. Sap does not only

CHAPTER FIVE UNSEEN SCALES

go up a tree[20] but it goes around in a spiral[41], as it goes up.

The *shape* of each plant, or stationary form of life, is established by the boundaries of its vortex or its field, or its aura[61],. Everything everywhere is encompassed in such an auric field[61].

In life that moves, such as animals, the soul force in the body establishes form from the central, intelligent, master cell. This frequency of the animals is much lower than the human form, of course.

The animal body of humans is the manifested filler, composed of inert matter, that is required in the frequency upon the Earth's[10] surface. The soul force is distributed through the inert matter by the blood stream. The Man body of Reality establishes the "field".

In climbing a hill you have to push the vortex upward. It is much easier for some people to so climb than others. This is because their polarity balance is nearer to neutrality. If the physical, negative vortex, surrounded by the aura, reaches a balance between what we term "spirit" and the "physical", that person can climb a hill without effort because it is not required that he push the inert matter upward in defiance of the laws of gravity.

The human vortices also start and end at the surface of the ground. In man, balance is achieved above the Earth's[10] surface. The negative vortex has its apex downward, at the feet. The positive vortex of the Real body has its apex upward, above the head.

CHAPTER FIVE UNSEEN SCALES

When the balance between the physical reflection and the real body, or the consciousness of your Being[58] reaches a state of equilibrium, these vortices will be of the same length, the same diameter, and the same speed of rotation. You can levitate yourself with the forces established at a zero point between these <u>two opposing polarities</u>[30].

Through these vortices, and with them you can establish a "field" of protection around you. Not necessarily by willful direction but by the actions you manifest. If your thought is good your actions are of a giving nature; if you are concerned with the welfare of others you automatically establish a "field" of protection around you because the Universal Mind[64] compensates directly, and equally, for every thought and action.

The zero balance between the physical vortex and the vortex of the Real, conscious, everlasting You, is difficult to hold. You may be unbalanced slightly in one direction or the other; in one belief or the other; in the manifested actions you perform.

The purpose in your being on the surface of the planet is to bring about a balance, first, in your own control, and next, a balance between each of you; an understanding, a compassion, a love that is not expressed in words. This balance cannot be maintained mechanically, for you don't know which vortex to increase, or decrease. But by following the basic principle of the *Golden Rule*[62], by doing all things in moderation, you will arrive at a point of equilibrium where you will be able to know which side of zero you must bring

CHAPTER FIVE   UNSEEN SCALES

up, or down. When you reach a state of zero polarity between your individual vortices, you are at One with th.e infinite Mind. You can know anything, you can see anything, and you can be anything of your own choice, so long as you maintain that balance.

If you associate closely with people, these vortices can leak; thereby causing you to acquire disease or character conditions of ones you associate with.

This is also responsible for what we call. Love. Not the real love, but the physical attraction of one for another, oftentimes of one sex for the same sex. If one has a predominantly negative, physical vortex and another has a predominantly spiritual vortex, these two vortices are attracted to each other. This is not the condition of love. It is a condition of mutual attraction by two people, who may seem to be entirely opposite in every other respect.

Someone at a distance from you cannot affect you, but in close association you will assimilate characteristics of another person. These are natural things, because nature wants to balance everything. The spiritual person is attracted to the predominant materialist, and vice-versa.

The leakage of vortices is something you should watch for. You oan assimilate character, understanding, and love by association with people who demonstrate these characteristics. Therefore you should try to associate with these types of .people. The vortex of the human physical body will also cause people to be repelled. Oftentimes you will meet one whom you immediately dislike intensely. This is not a condition of knowing the other person; it is a natural condirtion of polarities repelling each other.

CHAPTER FIVE   UNSEEN SCALES

These things are beyond the scale. of records, as far as individuals go. It is not possible to compute, and understand, the vortices of all individuals.

Individually however; you can try to understand your own, and the effects of the vortices of other people upon you.

But remember, one can be close to you and discharge your vortex by an opposite charge, thereby causing you to feel physically tired and drained of life.

Study your friends at a safe distance (about six feet) before you associate closer, or you may discover what you term an enemy in the friendship you thought was yours.

0 man, My Light is not for the victor nor for the one who falls in defeat; My Light is to the one who gains understanding of My ways. My arms are not extended either to the right or the left, but are centered to balance the living individual parts of My Being. Though forces may oppose your every move, My strength lies in the power to meet the opposition. Though evil may tempt you, My Light is brightest when the evil is overcome. For evil is not of My creation, 0 man. Evil is brought about by those who falter on the way to Me. Never, never in all My eternity shall man control the paths to Me. The paths are My ways, and man can only travel on My paths. In all My doings I have brought about a pattern of progression. None can turn about My works, none can interrupt My way. Those who follow in the darkness only trip themselves. Stand within the Light of Me; for I am Light of thee, O man; and I can only shine when you have made the way in progress of My doing. Lean not upon another, only accept thy brother as one to help one to assist along the way,

CHAPTER FIVE   UNSEEN SCALES

that unity in numbers may bring about progress in My infinite Light. Fear not, fear not! There is no fear within My Being of you. Fear is only added by the things you do that are not within the pattern of My ways. Reach within, I am there. None can scare you when you find the Me in thee. Stand, stand upright. Death is only that which adds to those who have performed the grade. Fear no evil, stand within My Light. Feel My living Light within you. Know that I am there throughout eternity.

CHAPTER SIX   THE ANGELS OF SPACE

CHAPTER SIX

THE ANGELS[63] OF SPACE

"And the angel[63] that talked with me came again, and waked me, as a man that is wakened. out of his sleep." (Zechariah 4:.1).

This paragraph fits almost exactly the expeience that I had on August 24th of 1953.

Angels[63] were always considered by me to be some vaporus type of afterlife that just floated about here and there. My entire concept of things changed with the physically manifested appearance of one of these angels[63] to me.

From the position of the full Moon, I judged it to be around 2 A.M. Here on the desert it is nearly as bright in full moonlight as it is in daylight. I awakened, not knowing why; but sensing that something had happened that had disturbed me. We sleep outside about six months out of the year, so you can see that our bedroom was readily accessable.

As I looked up from the bed I saw a man standing about six feet away from the foot of the bed. This was not uncommon, as we operate a public airport and have been awakened many times by our dogs barking at people coming in during the night. However, at this time not a sound was heard from the dogs. This I recalled later and it was certainly unusual.

I asked the man what he wanted, thinking his car might have

CHAPTER SIX THE ANGELS OF SPACE

given him trouble and he had walked into our remote aiirfield as many others have done before. At the same time I sat up in bed. Beyond the man, about a hundred yards away, hovered a glittering, glowing spaceship[18], seemingly about eight feet off the ground.

I knew then that he was not having car trouble. The man said, "My name is Solgonda[63,64]. I would be pleased to show you our craft."

My left hand and arm were still under the covers. I pinched my wife in the side to awaken her. Solgonda[63,64] smiled, like he knew what I was doing. I pinched her again. she normally awakens very easily. I didn't want her to miss what was taking place. Solgonda smiled again. Still no response from my wife, so I pinched her hard. Solgonda[63,64] nearly laughed aloud. My wife didn't wake up and somehow I realized Solgonda[63,64] had her under some kind of control.

I hopped out of bed clad only in under-shorts. Solgonda[63,64] preceeded me for a few yards and then I caught up with him and walked beside him. Not a word was said as we walked to the ship. In fact, I never said another word to him.

From the time I got out of bed, until I returned to it, every time I thoughtt of something to say he was answering me before I could speak the first word of any sentence. This proved to me. their perfect ability to <u>communicate by thought transference</u>[8].

As we approched the craft I began to get butterflies in my

CHAPTER SIX   THE ANGELS OF SPACE

stomach from about fifty feet away. Coming nearer, my hair seemed to want to stand up on end. This feeling disappeared instantly upon entering the ship[39].

The craft was about 36 feet in diameter and about 19 feet high. It looked like the same type that George Adamski[65] photographed in his close-ups.

The interior was about 18 feet in diameter and about 10 feet high. The walls were of some opalescent material like our imitation mother of pearl. There was a shelf around the inside below the portholes, about elbow height from the floor when one was standing. A column extended from the ceiling to the floor in the center of the ship[39].

Three[56]. other men were on the craft when we went in. They were all of the same approximate height of Solgonda[63,64], who was about 5 feet 7 inches tall. These three men smiled but never spoke, and I didn't learn their names.

Solgonda demonstrated their retractable seats, which formed a lounge when extended out of the walls. He showed me several celestial navigation instruments, and then we went below the main deck through a manhole into the power generating room.

Below the deck it was necessary to crouch down on a circular catwalk. There the power mechanism was exposed to view, and I understood the principle of operation, which Solgonda[63,64] apparently picked up by "telethought[8]".

We left the ship after what I judged to be 20 minutes.

CHAPTER SIX THE ANGELS OF SPACE

Solgonda[63,64] walked back to bed with me, where my wife was peacefully sleeping. When I climbed back in bed I wondered if the strange feeling I had had in my stomach was going to affect me in any way. Before I could put the thought into .words Solgonda[63,64] said, "No, you,ll be all right", and instantly disappeared.

About a minute latter the ship slipped slowly into the sky and was out of sight in less than a minute.

Later we checked the hovering spot with a magnetic compass. The vortex set up by the field from the ship would swing the needle 10° easterly in walking into the vortex center, and 5° westerly in passing out of the center on the opposite side. People who went there a week later to eat their lunch became nauseated and couldn't eat.

I know now that angels are people that come out of space. They not only colonize planets and <u>communicate by thought</u>[8], but they spend their time helping other people to understand Life. Right now they are 'around and on our planet to help humanity out of the mess we have gotten ourselves into.

People are people everywhere in the Creator's[16] universe[7]. The only difference is that most of them have followed the universal laws[60] and thereby progressed, while we on Earth[10] have not. You had a body before you came here on Earth[10] and you'll have another one when you leave. But maybe then you'll be called an angel. Genesis tells of God[11] making Man, but it doesn't say anything about Him making angels[63,64]. This further proved to me that angels[63,64] are the race of Man.

CHAPTER SIX THE ANGELS OF SPACE

The first mention of an angel in the Bible comes in Genesis 16 :7. In this verse the angel[63,64] is referred to as "an angel[63,64] of the Lord[11]".

The sages of Biblical times knew the mysteries and actions of the esoteric laws. Thus it was known to them that everything that was motivated by natural forces traveled in an arc, or curved path. Anything that moved in any other path of motion was unnatural and was symbolically termed an "angle". People living in Abram's[15] time therefore referred to anything that was of an unnatural motion from their point of view on the Earth's[11] surface, as an "angle".

These people didn't know anything about weather baloons, modem airplanes, land high flying jets. The only things they knew of 'that flew in the sky were winged birds.

When they observed a spacecraft, or men come out of the sky, they naturally pictured them with wings, like the birds.

Since the appearance of men or ships in the sky was not a naturally happening occurrence, they symbolized the sky visitors as "angles[63,64]".

The way these people recorded any happening was to have one of their scribes write it down. Like a newspaper reporter of today who wasn't present at the actual scene, the scribe had to write it as it was described to him by eyewitnesses.

Whenever the people wanted a copy of any written record, they found a scribe to copy it for them. The scribes of those

CHAPTER SIX   THE ANGELS OF SPACE

days got things twisted as badly as the reporters and newspapers of today do.

Due to error in interpreting the symbol, the scribes in copying the accounts of the "angles" coming out of the skies wrote "angel", instead of "angle". All copies made from an erroneous one usually repeated the same mistake. So Angles became Angels[63,64].

In a number of the experiences describing contacts with the people in the spacecraft, the Earth[10] people making the contacts stated that the space people "disappeared" before their eyes.

As this also occurred to me during my contact I can understand their amazement. The uninformed would say they "dematerialized". The technically minded people would say "they went into the fourth dimension". The psychiatrist would say tha t the people suffered from hallucinations. *None of these are true.*

The reason our space friends can "disappear" is because our physical vision depends on light reflection off of things in order to see. The wave length of visible light extends from approximately 4000 Angstroms (extreme violet) to 7700 Angstroms (extreme red). Compared with the known radiation spectrum as a whole, the range of physical vision is *extremely* limited. This is comparable to looking at the landscape through a crack between two boards, and saying the landscape outside the range of visibility doesn't exist, has dematerialized, or is a hallucination.

Our space friends know LIGHT [66] inside out and backwards.

CHAPTER SIX   THE ANGELS OF SPACE

In order to eliminate the need for weapons which would injure others, they have developed what they call the "perfect defense".

This is a small object about two by two inches square and about one half inch thick. It has rounded comers and is generally carried on a cord around the neck and suspended under the blouse.

Their ability to read thoughts allows them to be aware of any danger or threat, and all they have to do is tap this device with either hand; and then appear to disappear.

The object is actually a "crystal battery" that stores "piezo" electricity that is generated by cutting magnetic lines of force, or the same as static electricity.

The nearest thing to this electricity stored by the "crystal battery" that we know of, we refer to as the "spirit body", or aura.

The electrical, spirit body of people varies with their environment, and the chemical make-up of their physical body. This is why you feel good when you are with some people, and feel drained, or exhausted, after association with others. Some people have stronger spirit bodies than others.

When the scoutship landed here in August of 1953, I observed this object. Solgonda was turning it by the corners between his hands. Suddenly he opened <u>two opposite ends</u>[25,30] of it and pointed it at the granite rocks of the mountain[20]. I saw a pencil-lead-size stream of light[66] between the object and the

CHAPTER SIX THE ANGELS OF SPACE

mountain[20]. I thought he was shooting something near the mountain[20]. Later he explained that he was charging the device. He said they charge various other pieces of their equipment over granite mountains. This is due to the piezo-electric effect set up by quartz in its granite matrix.

When they discharge the "crystal battery" by pressing on either side of it, it releases the charge into their electric body, or aura, and causes light to bend around them; therefore appearing to disappear to the limited physical vision of anyone who is watching them.

They do not dematerialize or go into any other dimension. They are just as solid and physical as always, but they are outside of the limits of physical vision.

This same device was used by the man Jesus when he "disappeared" out of crowds of people, and again when he "reappeared" unto the people after three[56] days.

In St. Luke 24:13-21, it tells how two of the people walked down the road talking with him[11].

Verse 31 says, "And their eyes were opened, and they knew him[11]; and *he[11] vanished out of their sight"*.

Some teachings would have you believe that this was a vision the people had. Jesus discounted this himself in St. Luke 24: 36-39 when he said, "handle me, and see; for a spirit hath not flesh and bones, as ye see me have".

Two women shall be grinding together; *the one shall be*

CHAPTER SIX   THE ANGELS OF SPACE

taken, and the other left. Two men shall be in the field; the *one shall be taken,* and the other one left. (St. Luke 17: 35, 36).

Either you have faith in the prophecy of the Bible, or you must reject the whole book. The Bible is an accurate history of events that repeat themselves in <u>cyclic repetition</u>[14].

The above paragraphs say a vision of humankind will be made. *One. shall be taken* and one shall be left.

Who is to make the decision? Who will do this judging of humanity to see who will be taken and who will be left?

Every day that passes, you, individually, are establishing your right to be taken *by the way you live.* You are manifesting your choice by your actions and thinking.

Each person adds increase to their vibratory body aura[61] by conforming to the <u>laws of the universe</u>[60]. Your aura[6], or the frequency of the body force field, will determine whether you are taken or left.

A definite vibration will be established in the force field surrounding each spacecraft[18] that will pick up people. If your body aura[61] or force field conforms with, or exceeds, the established level of thle spacecraft[18] force field, then you can enter the ships[39].

Remember, *you are now* qualifying or disqualifying *yourself* to be taken aboard. None can qualify another. Jesus can't

CHAPTER SIX THE ANGELS OF SPACE

"save" you. Some narrow-minded sects of religious fanatics have established that only 144,000 people will be saved. Of course *they* are part of the chosen few. Those who will be *taken,* and those who will be *saved,* are two separate conditions.

The next thing one asks is, "Where will the people who are picked up be taken?" This is answered in St. Luke 1 7 : 3 7. "And they answered and said unto him, Where, Lord? And he said unto them, Where so ever the *body* is, thither will the *eagles* be gathered together."

Naturally the eagles gather together in the sky. This was said in a parable at that time, because the people in the Biblical days didn't know what it was to fly in the skies. It was not meant for the people of those days. It was said for the people of *our time.*

The space people (angels[63,64]) explained that the people who have been taken aboard their craft[39] in these times, were not taken aboard because they were better than anyone else. They explained that these people were taken aboard for *their own test purposes;* to see how different types of people would react. Each one who has been so honored was readily accessible in a remote place. They were of cooperative minds, and each represented a different type of the Earth's[10] people.

This mass pickup of people will take place prior to the planet's rebalancing on new poles. This cataclysm will wipe out the destructive mammon lover who will be *left on the surface.*

CHAPTER SIX THE ANGELS OF SPACE

After the Earth[10] has re-stabilized on its new poles[37] and the continents and oceans have changed, then the people who have been taken up in the air will be landed back on the surface.

"Watch ye therefore, and pray always, that may be accounted worthy to escape all these thing that shall come to pass, and to stand before the *Son of man.*" (St. Luke 21: 36).

0 man, in the rings established within the Light of Me, orbiting My systems I am potency that moves a nebula, that causes suns to shine. Though some upon this portion of Myself have devious ways to violate My infinite Wisdom, it is not I who judge nor pay the price. As in My cycles, as in My phases, as in My eons, I have established precision in the order of My parts. And though a voice comes through to you unrecognized by mortals, realize, in the voice, I am the potent substance-force of Life, pulsing through your Being, unto eternity. I separate the white from black and color boundaries do I set, for all My creations are of Me, from lowest animal to tree, and all that is. I am the unseen force that manifests in everything you do. Impotent substance-clay of Me cannot interfere, except to bring about conditions that reflect upon the garment that you wear.

0 man, never shall you find an end to Me. There is no place I cannot be and am.

You make your hell by deeds you do in violation of My ways. One who says "hell is a place in My infinity", is violating Me.

Reaction is the only hell, rebounding from a spell when you excluded Me, 0 man!

CHAPTER SIX   THE ANGELS OF SPACE

Some preach there is a hell for others, never for themselves. Watch out for these their eg.o is leading them astray.

Through space and time and place, remember I am there and here with you.

I have no hell for man of Me. Man who believes there is a hell, is reviving imagery of experiences he has had along the road to Me.

CHAPTER SEVEN PRODIGAL MOTHER

CHAPTER SEVEN

PRODIGAL[67] MOTHER[10]

The levels. or strata of substance around the crust of the Earth[10] are separated by insulations of the One Still Light[66]. These layers of insulation are the activalting Intelligence of the Creator[16] in relation to our planet. Intelligence infiltrates all of the matter in the substance strata. Each alternate matter strata is of opposite polarity[30] and rotates opposite to the matter strata on each side of it.

The Earth[10] is a battery; the strata are the plates. God[11] separates and centers all things through the "G" lines of Still Light[66]. He activates all things through the "A" positive, and "B" negative lines of force.

The center of our planet consists of a sun[29]. This sun[29], as the core, rotates in the opposite direction to the moving crust.

Between the fiery center of the positively charged core and the negative crust is an insulating, nonconductive strata of fluid glass (obsidian), six hundred miles in thickness.

All ruptures of the crust are caused by *atmospheric* conditions. There are several well-defined areas on the surface of the Earth where vortices of magnetic ,energy are located. In due time these vortices will bring about. the

CHAPTER SEVEN   PRODIGAL MOTHER

rupture of the crusttermed volcanic action. The earthquake[53] faults were brought about by interruptions of the force field around the Earth[10] .

Planets without moisture in their atmosphere do not rotate. As the "A" and "B" lines of force enter the atmosphere and the crust of the planet, parallel to the Equator and at 90° from each ather and the axis, they spiral to each pole and arrive there before the planet has made one quarter of a turn. Emitting from the poles, they encounter resistance in the form of uninterrupted "A" and "B" lines of force, bringing about the phenomena termed aurora[68] .

Every planet in the universe moves in curved lines of travel. This is not because they were thrown off by a sun[29], or central body. If they were, they would not orbit. Anything thrown off of a rotating object will travel in a str.aight line outward, though on the Earth[10] . it may fall because of gravity.The reason planets or electrons orbit around a central body is because they are powered by light energy.

Space outside of the Earth's[10] atmosphere is blacker than the blackest ink. Our Sun[29] looks like any other bright star, not like a ball of fire. Only the brightest stars can be seen.

Pictured in the drawing is what has often been termed "the four dark comers". The Positive Quarter, or Spring Season of the Earth's[10] . orbit, is only predominantly positive relative to the Earth's[10] . passing through it. At all other times when light energy is not interrupted by a body or planet, the negative or

CHAPTER SEVEN PRODIGAL MOTHER

Drawing 5

CHAPTER SEVEN   PRODIGAL MOTHER

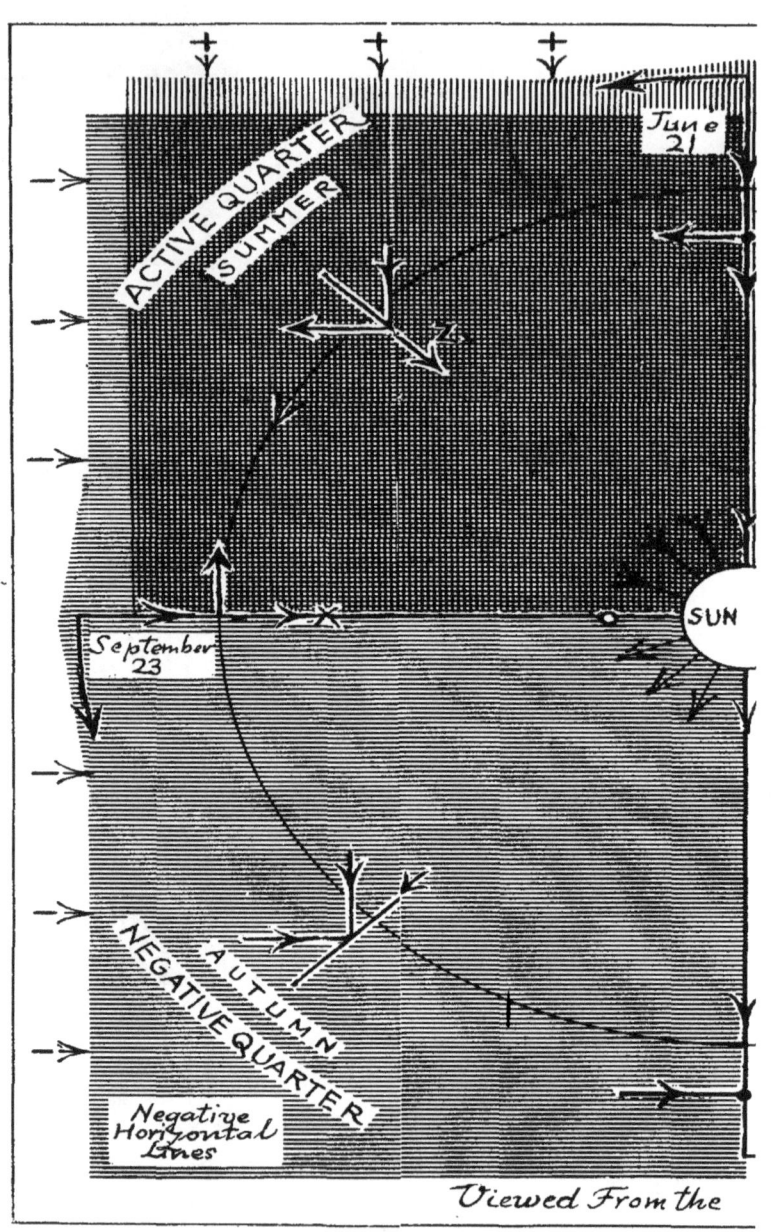

CHAPTER SEVEN PRODIGAL MOTHER

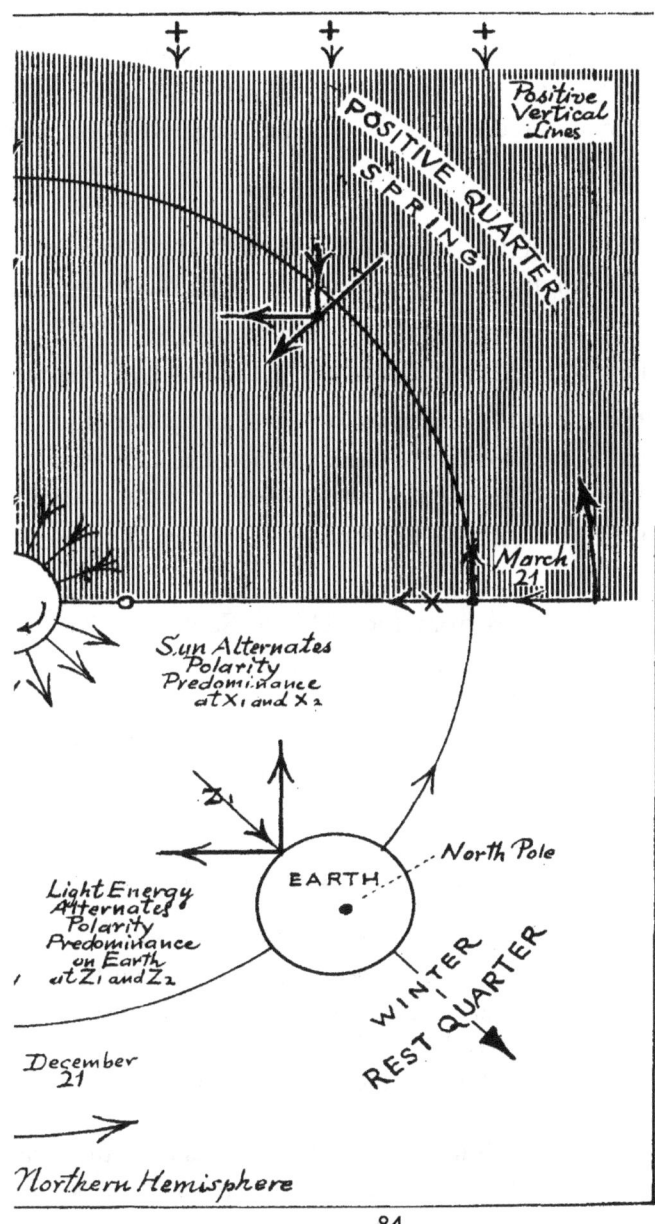

CHAPTER SEVEN PRODIGAL MOTHER

female lines of fotce predominate. The old axiom "women first" is applicable throughout the universe. *As* the Sun crosses the Earth's Equator on March 21, it affects a positively charged cyclic predominance in the negative northern hemisphere.

In the arc from <u>March 21 to September 23</u>[69] , the Sun tries to attract the Earth to it. This causes the negatively charged Earth[10] to describe the arc of its orbit from <u>March 21</u>[69] to June 21. This is noted in the drawing as the Positive Quarter. The reason the Earth[10] proceeds toward the negative lines of light energy in the Positive Quarter, is because the negative lines of light energy have been weakened from passing through the Sun's[29] force field, or positively charged vortex.

As the Earth[10] moves from June 21[70] to September 23[69], it starts in the downward direction of its elliptical arc. This is called the Active Quarter. These conditions are being viewed from the northern hemisphere in this explanation. In the southern hemisphere the Active and Rest Quarters would be opposite from those shown here.

As the negatively charged Earth[10] follows its path in the Active Quarter, it is attracted by the positive Sun[29] on the negative northern hemisphere and by the   negative lines of light energy which are acting on the positive southern hemisphere. The positive lines of light energy are repelling on the positively predominant southern hemisphere.

The Active Quarter is Summer, our hottest season of the year. This heat is caused by the increase in resistance, set up

CHAPTER SEVEN PRODIGAL MOTHER

gradually by the Sun[29] extending its path on the Earth[10] laterally 1:0 its northernmost extreme. In the daytime it is hotter because the Sun[29] is farther into the negative northern hemisphere, thereby setting up more resistance in our negatively charged atmosphere and the negatively charged crust of the negative hemisphere. At the midway point between June 21[70] and September 23[69], the Earth[10] also reaches its maximum exposure to the resistance of both the positive and negative lines of light energy. This increase in resistance from all three forces at the same time generates more heat.

As the Earth[10] proceeds in its path from September 23[69] to December 21[70], the days become shorter as the Sun[29] starts changing from the Equator into the positively charged southern hemisphere.

The positive Sun's[29] effect on a positive hemisphere repels the planet. The negatively charged light lines of energy predominate and repel the planet from their direction of travel, causing it to arc through its orbit to December 21[70].

From December 21[70] to March 21[69] the negative predominance of the lines of light energy are again decreasing and at "Z" in the Rest Quarter all forces reach balance for an instant. *At* "Z" in the Rest Quarter the field or vortex of the Sun decreases both the positive and negative lines of light energy. The Sun[29] has reached 'a half-way point between the Equator and its southernmost lateral extreme. Then the positive lines of light energy begin to attract the negatively

CHAPTER SEVEN PRODIGAL MOTHER

charged planet and the increasing predominance of the negatively charged northern hemisphere. The Sun[29] begins to attract the increasing negative predominance of the planet and the negative lines of light energy begin to repel the increasing negative predominance of the northern hemisphere.

The Sun[29] and all of our planets are moving through space in the direction indicated by the arrow in the Rest Quarter of the drawing. Everything in the universe is trying to reach balance by traveling in the Rest Quarter direction.

The fact that the Earth[10] has more land-mass in the northern hemisphere than in the southern hemisphere is the reason for the Earth's[10] orbit being slightly elliptical. Land sets up more polarity action than water. The Sun[29] acts upon the predominance of the polarity of the hemisphere presented to it by the Equinox[69] alternation.

At <u>March 21 and September 23</u>[69], both the northern and the southern hemispheres are attracted and repelled equally and oppositely for an instant by the Sun[29].

The Sun[29] reaches its maximum attraction on the Earth on June 21[70] and repels at its maximum on December 21[70].

The light lines of positive and negative energy act upon the Earth[10] as an alternating, negatively charged body. The Sun[29] acts upon the oppositely polarized hemispheres as they are presented to it in the seasons.

CHAPTER SEVEN PRODIGAL MOTHER

The relative increase or decrease in polarity action varies continuously, depending upon the tilt of the Earth[10], the resistance of the Sun's[29] force field, and effects of the quarterly cycles upon each succeeding Cycle.

People have less resistance to disease in Winter, because at that quarter of the Earth's[10] orbit the life light lines of energy are reduced due to passing through the rotating vortex of the Sun's[29] force field.

Any change of polarity predominance in the Earth's[10] atmosphere or crust will result in climatic changes. This is how positively charged particles from Hydrogen bombs have caused weather changes and exttremes throughout the world.

Our atmospheric strata is only a thin layer of gases and moisture emitted from the crust. Our frequent charging of the atmosphere with radioactive substances is a slow process of self-annihilation. The temperature drop noted after each atomic bomb blast is caused by the inrush of frigid air from higher strata. If 30 atomic bombs were exploded in 30 days, our Earth[10] population would be forced undergroud by the extreme cold.

0 man, I expand the buds in the springtime of My seasons. I bring forth hues of colors in · the sun-sets. I breathe forth fragrance from the flowers. I build a nest. I surge with Joy and Love, that you may grow in Unity and compassion. I bring about the warmth of My breath in the season of My summers that man may know the fullness of the harvest, that man may see the repetition of My doings in examples all about him. And then I bring the cold, I change My colors. I

CHAPTER SEVEN PRODIGAL MOTHER

cool My breath the leaves of Me fall to nourish the soil, that once again I may come in the fullness of My springtime. And then I breathe My holy breath through . naked branches in the blast of winter. I crown My mountains with the purity of whiteness, in mantles of snow. I freeze My rivers so that man may know the change that comes about in the seasons of My densities. I blast the breath of storm, and then I tire of cold and bring My seasons and cycles into repetition. My numberless worlds are there for man. The mysteries are 'there at hand to see, so man may know the Me in thee. When he solves the problems of My doing then I shall know he will grow in Me; he will know with Me eternity.

This same principle of light energy maintains the Earth's[10] cycles of day and night, temperature, tides, and the relation and effects of the Moon[50] on the Earth[10] and her people.

The Sun[29] does not emit light of itself. The Sun[29] transmits positively polarized force which reacts upon the Earth[10] because of its negative polarity.

The Moon[50] is one of the bodies acting as a governor to the Earth[10]. The Earth's tides are a "fluid drive" connection between the motor-generator-battery Earth[10], and the governor Moon[50].

Gravity of the Moon[50] has no effect upon the Earth[10]. The only effect of the Moon[50] upon the Earth is by polarity action on the Earth's[10] force field, and by intetruption of the light lines of force.

CHAPTER SEVEN PRODIGAL MOTHER

Drawing 6

CHAPTER SEVEN PRODIGAL MOTHER

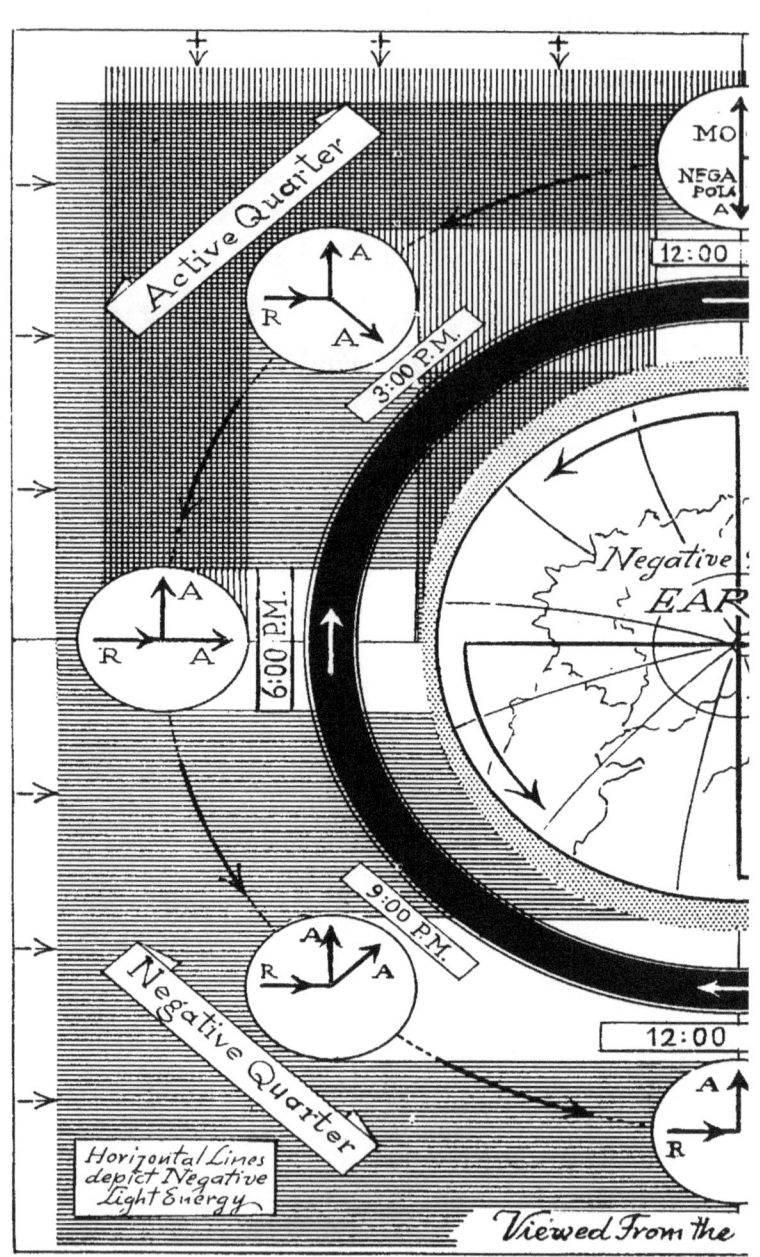

CHAPTER SEVEN PRODIGAL MOTHER

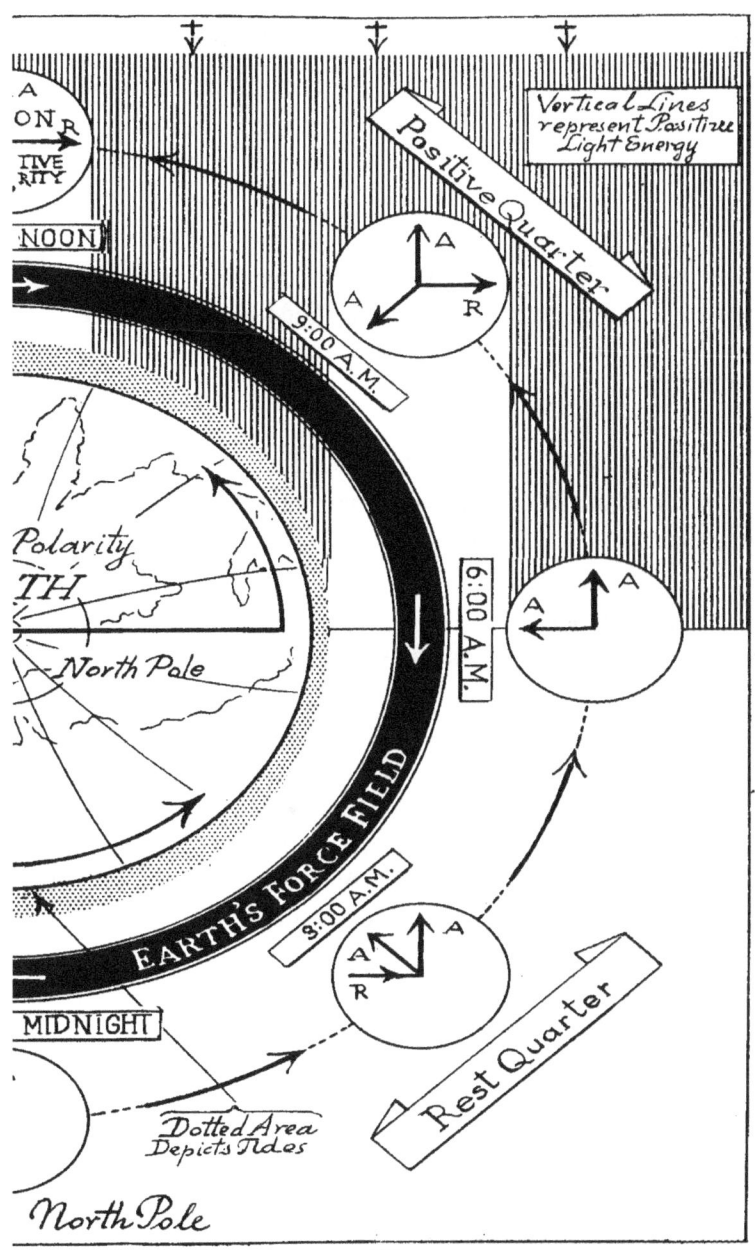

CHAPTER SEVEN PRODIGAL MOTHER

The Earth[10] is surrounded by a self-generated force field. Nothing inside of the Earth's[10] force field is affected by anything outside of it, except through the attracting or repelling effects of polarity in the lines of light energy, or the Sun[29].

Gravity. within the force field generated by any body is not subject to the action of any body outside of the force field; unless the body outside of the force field is of opposite polarity.

The Moon[50] and the Earth[10] are both of negative polarity, as are all humans in their physical substance and all bodies that can be seen by reflected light[66].

All negative bodies generate a positive force field and all positively charged bodies generate a negative force field.

Temperature is the result of light forces acting in opposition to each other. Magnetism is an effect of primary light[66] energy in opposition, produced as a result of its interruption by any body. Electricity is an effect of magnetism in polarity opposition. Heat is an effect of electricity in opposition. Contraction and expansion are opposite effects of heat, or the lack of it.

The Earth's[10] force field is the boundary of everything inside of it. Nothing can come into it or go out through it without conforming to its positive polarity.

The space people can alternate the polarity of the force field

CHAPTER SEVEN   PRODIGAL MOTHER

around their ships to conform to the positive polarity of the Earth's[10] force field while they are passing through it.

The Moon[50] never was hurled from the Earth; and it will never be part of the Earth, due to the Earth's force field.

Let us start in the Positive Quarter and rotate the Moon[50] around the Earth[10].

The small arrows shown on the Moon[50] indicate the direction of forces set up by polarity affecting the Moon. The "A" arrows represent attractive forces and the "R" arrows stand for repelling forces. At all times these forces are changing their predominance, which establishes the Moon's orbit around the Earth[10]. The Moon's[50] orbit speed is fixed according to its charge of negative polarity.

The secondary light . rays from the positive Sun[29] and the positive lines of, light energy warm the morning cycle from 6 A.M. to 12 Noon. This occurs by the attractive, resistance heat-effect in our negative atmosphere and crust of the Earth[10]. The force field does not decrease these polarity effects ecause their polarities are bath, positive, therefore they offer no resistance to each other.

The heat registered during the hottest part of the day is in the Active Quarter from 12 Noon to 6 P.M. Higher temperartures are registered in this quarter because the Sun[29] and positive lines of light energy are setting up attraction resistance within our atmosphere, and the negative lines of light energy are setting up repelling resistane. Two forces are working in

CHAPTER SEVEN PRODIGAL MOTHER

attraction to the Earth's[10] polarity and one force is working in opposition to it. The negative lines of force also meet resistance of the positive force field, which acts as a reflector.

From 6 P.M to Midnight is the. Negative Quarter. Both the positive lines of light energy and the Sun's[29] attractive forces are eliminated and the negative lines of light[66] energy maintain only the heat of resistance by repulsion. The forces of the Active Quarter fade away and the negative physical bodies of people become tired and sleepy during the Negative Quarter.

In the Rest Quarter from Midnight to 6 A.M., the Sun's positive force, the positive lines of light energy, and the negative lines of light[66] energy set up no resistance of attractive or repelling forces. So the atmosphere and crust cool off in the coldest quarter of the cycle, because the Earth[10] is shielded from the three forces. For the same reason more people die from "natural causes" in the Rest Quarter than in the other three quarters combined. This is because their "physical resistance" is low. In other words, none of the three life forces of light[66] are active in the physical body during the Rest Quarter. That is what rest is the lack of polarity opposition forces. Everything is meant to rest in the Rest Quarter and all of nature does it, except in cases where the positive polarity is predominant.

People of a predominantly negative polarity cannot stand to work on a "graveyard shift". People of a predominantly positive polarity are ofen called lazy because their Active Quarter and Rest Quarter reactions are opposite and they want to sleep in the daytime.

CHAPTER SEVEN PRODIGAL MOTHER

Drawing 7

CHAPTER SEVEN   PRODIGAL MOTHER

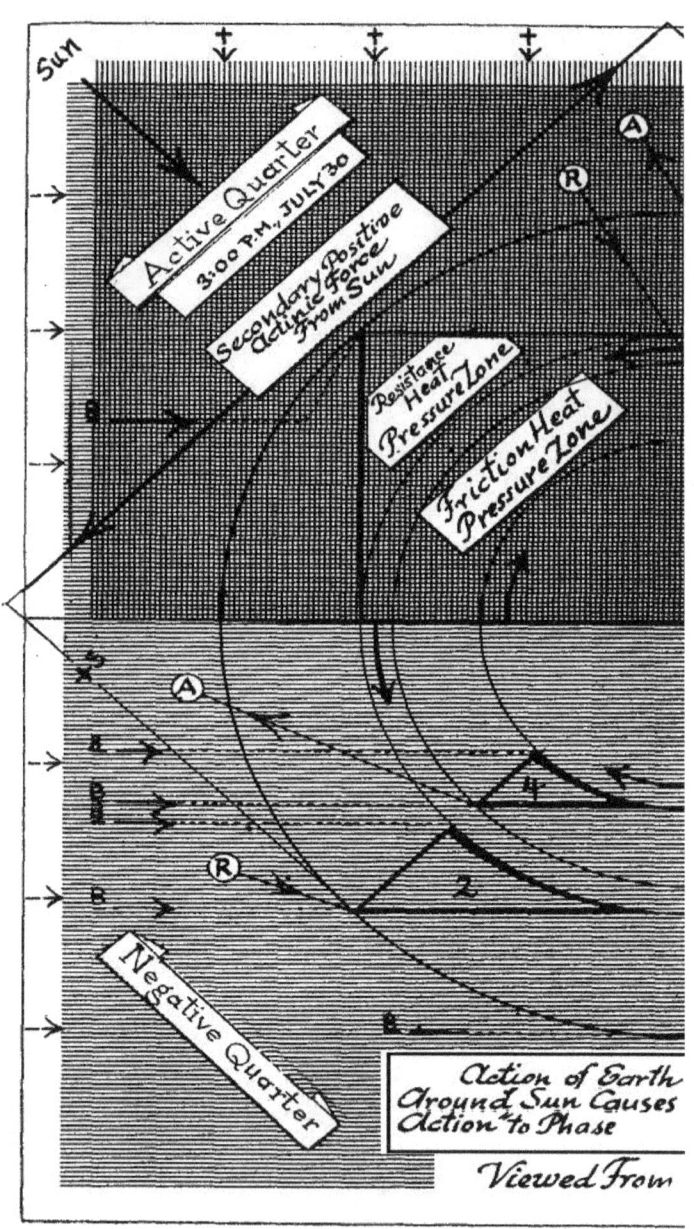

CHAPTER SEVEN PRODIGAL MOTHER

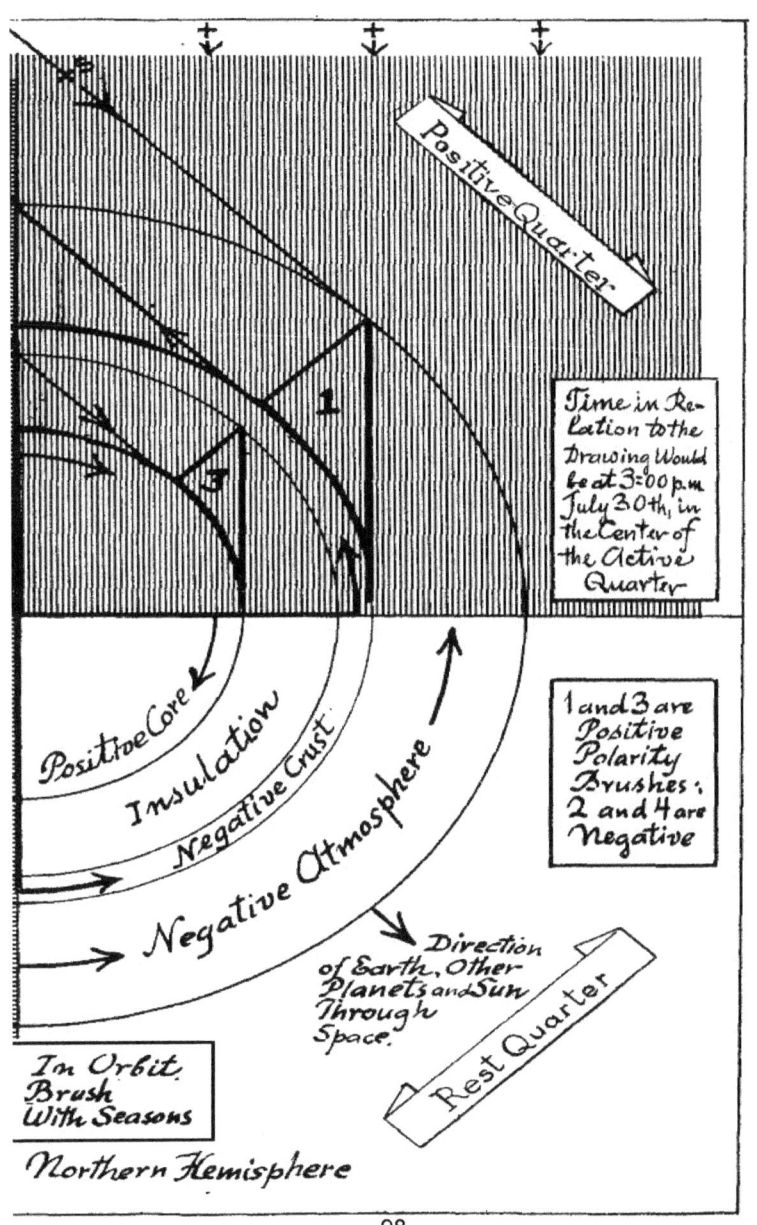

CHAPTER SEVEN   PRODIGAL MOTHER

It has been maintained by science that the Moon[50] causes the tides. This is not so any more than the profession that heat comes from the Sun[11].

The polarity predominance alternates between the northern and southern hemispheres of the Earth[10] and causes the force field to oscillate. The erratic orbit path of the Moon[50] follows the oscillations of the Earth's[10] force field. The Eartth's[10] positive force field rotates opposite to I the Earth and the Moon's[50] orbit. Interruptions of the light lines of force by other bodies or planets causes variable effects on the Earth[10] and its reactions are transmitted to its ' self-generated force field.

The Earth's[10] force field causes the tides, as it is of opposite polarity to the water. The fact that it is strongest at the point of most resistance where the Moon[50] is, explains the reason that science profeses that the Moon attracts the water, causing the tides. A negative Moon[50] cannot attract a negative body of water; it would repel the water[48] and in that case the tides would be lowest on the Earth[10] on the side toward the Moon[50].

The cyclic interruption by the Moon[50] between the positive and negative lines of light energy and the Earth[10], is what causes diurnal inequalities in the four tides of a day and the age of the tide. Water[48] being a fluid accounts for the equal

CHAPTER SEVEN PRODIGAL MOTHER

effect on the opposite side of the Earth[10]. The fact that the force field is rotating in the opposite direction to the Earth[10] and is strongest at a point between the greatest resistance of atraction by both the Earth[10] and the Moon[50], is what causes the "tides to lag"; a fact which has never been explained satisfactorily by science.

Magnetism in and around the Earth[10] is a result of the Earth's[10] interruption of the lines of primary light[66] energy. Electricity is the result of interruption of the Earth's[10] magnetism by a generator.

As the lines of primary light energy are in motion, any body that interrupts them will move according to its capacity and polarity charge.

Electricity is the second by-product of primary light energy; magnetism is the first. Neither can exist without the other because they are both part of each other.

In the drawing we show only the positively charged core of the Earth[10], the insulation, the negative crust, and the negative atmosphere. Actually these charged strata and insulating layers extend to strata around Mars and Venus.

The drawing is made with the Sun[29] shining in the center of the Active Quarter from a 45 o angle. The Sun[29] is the alternator that changes polarity predominance from one hemisphere to the other every six[71] months.

CHAPTER SEVEN   PRODIGAL MOTHER

The "A" and "R" circles indicate the direction of the attracting and repelling forces. The negative primary light attracts the positive core in the Negative Quarter and repels the negative crust. The opposite is true in the Positive Quarter. These attracting and repelling "brushes" are changing position continuously as the Earth[10] orbits.

The atmosphere is actually a part of the crust and is of the same polarity. It acts as a bearing for the crust to turn in. The atmosphere and oceans are affected by the helical vortex set up in each hemisphere, which rotate in opposite directions. This is caused by the depleted lines of primary light[66] giving their energy to cause motion of the planet. As they are depleted they try to reach rest, so they had for the points of least motion; which is at the poles. Naturally polarity seeks opposite polarity[30,31] always.

A compass needle does not point to the north magnetic pole because it is attracted to it by an opposite polarity. Its negative charged end is only pressed into position parallel to the lines of light force going by it. The intelligence in the molecular arrangement of its negative charge wants to go with the other positively charged light lines in motion around it. For the same reason the negative Earth[10], or our other planets were never part of the positive Sun[29]. The planets being of opposite polarity could be attracted to it, but never thrown off from the Sun[29].

The Sun's[29] insulation stratum prevents the positive polarity of the Sun[29] from attracting the negative Earth[10] into it.

CHAPTER SEVEN   PRODIGAL MOTHER

Light[66] is transmitted into energy by penetration into the matter that interrupts it. The matter then gains motion.

A negative vortex of light energy produces decelerating effects in negative matter. A positive vortex of light energy produces accelerating effects in negative matter.

You can apply the principle of the Earth's[10] crust and core rotation in opposite directions to an electric motor.

Mount both ends of the shaft on fixed bearings. These bearings will suspend the entire motor.

Run the two wires from the motor case to two copper rings mounted on insulation, on one end of the shaft, inside the fxed bearing. Bruhes from the power supply must contact the two rings.

Be sure to remove the base of the motor and balance the field case on the fixed bearings.

Power applied will rotate the armature in one direction and the field case in the other direction, at different speeds.

By applying a pulley to the shaft and another to the case, then running "V" belt from both pulleys to a common point of work, the torque force of the normal base type electric motor will also be applied to the work.

One "V" belt will have to be twisted 180 degrees between the motor pulley and the pulley of the work, to counteract the opposite rotations. in the Motor. This uses the torque force to do useful work, reduces speed and wear on the bearings, and

CHAPTER SEVEN   PRODIGAL MOTHER

furnishes more power for greater work output.

This is the same way the core and crust of the. Earth[10] function, *each being a balance to the other.* The crust[72] is the field and the core[72] is the armature.

Unfortunately, the explosion of kiloton and megaton power "A" and "H" bombs have unbalanced natural conditions. This will bring about a steady increase in subterranean temperatures in the northern hemisphere, and lowering of temperatures in the southern hemisphere. The rapid <u>shifting of the magnetic poles</u>[37] registered on the surface is the result of these bombs unbalancing the planet. Wherever the magnetic poles on the negative polarity surface are found, *they indicate where the axis of the positive polarity core*[72] *is located under the crust*[72].

The core is encased in fluid obsidian 600 miles thick. Oscillations of the core, which were set up by the reaction to the bomb forces, will cause an increase in volcanoes and earthquakes, due to increased frictional heat in tthe fluid separator.

Throw the fine balance of the electric motor case out, and see what would happen to the armature if it were floating in a fluid. Any spinning giroscope will wobble if it is moved from its plane of rotation. The Earth[10] works like a gyroscope. Magnets, atoms, planets, and people all have polarities of either positive, or negative predominance.

Because a body pedominates in one polarity does not mean

CHAPTER SEVEN   PRODIGAL MOTHER

that the substance of its composition does not include matter of the opposite polarity. When your positive polarity body reaches predominance your negative polarity physical body dies.

The same thing applies to planets, magnets, or atomic structure.

The nuclear (positive polarity) devices being exploded in our negative polarity atmosphere are rapidly bringing about a condition of polar change on the Earth's[10] surface. The emission of positive polarity particles (fallout) from the "H" bomb tests are unbalancing the polarity predominance of the Earth[10].

The positive fallout particles are attracted to the negative polarity, north magnetic pole. When the positive particles fall there on negative polarity ice the resistance causes heat, causing the ice to melt.

The negartive polarity water released by melting is repelled by the more predominantly negative polarity crust of the Earth[10] into a less predominantly negative polarity atmosphere.

In the air it is attracted in a spiral course to the positively predominant southern hemisphere, where most of it is attracted to the positive polarity, south magnetic pole.

This causes ice to build up at the southern pole and meltt the northern pole, bringing unbalance to the planet's axis indirectly from the explosion of nuclear bombs.

CHAPTER SEVEN PRODIGAL MOTHER

The magnetic poles registered on the-surface of the Earth's[10] crust[72] are in reality the axis poles of the Earth's positive polarity core. As more bomb tests transmute negative polarity matter to a positive polarity condition, the effects can be registered in many ways.

The magnetic declination shown on the Los Angeles (R-2) Sectional Aeronautical Chart, dated March 10, 1953, shows the 15° E. magnetic declination line at 115° 50' W. Longitude at the 34° N. Latitude line. The chart dated September 27, 1955, shows a shift of the 15° E. magnetic declination to 117° 2' W. This is a change of 1° 12' in 2½ years, or 28.8' per year. Formerly it was slightly over 9' per year.

The main reason for low layers of smog over most of the big cities is because the carbon particles in the air are not repelled upward as they used to be before the advent of "H" bomb tests. The polarity of these particles notmally being negative, they are becoming less negative due to the fact that carbon assimilates radioactivity of positive polarity; thus the repelling action is reduced and the particles hang closer to the surface instead of rising to be dispersed by the winds at higher altitudes.

Magnetism is the positive and negative fields generated by the revolving planet interrupting the positive and negative lines of primary energy present in all space. Electricity is the force generated by an armature interrupting the positive and negative lines of magnetism. Each has its effect on the other, and can be converted into the other.

The "time" field separates all primary polarities, all magnetic polarities, and all electrical polarities. This "time" field is

CHAPTER SEVEN PRODIGAL MOTHER

unseen, infinite, and maintains the balance between the opposite charges present in all bodies. This balance is manifest in all new creations.

With the continual testing of nuclear devices the planet's unbalance will increase by the equal and opposite reaction of polarities coming ever closer to balance.

This will bring about more ionizatin of the atmosphere, with an increase in smog, humidity, and clouds. Then the Bible prophecy will be fulfilled that says, "The Sun will no longer give forth her Light"

In the pattern of My ways I live My life in many forms, known *and unknown to other parts of Me. I live in space of Me to constantly supervise My doings; I live in soil to nourish My roots. I am the sap, the blood; in every density I am. I live My life and love it too, being the living Love of you, thrilling when you express the Me in thee.*

My life is sad only when you are mad at other parts of Me. Only when you manifest hate destroy; then 1 wait patiently for you to recover, to discover that *you have only injured Me and Thee.*

Your ever fight is My fight too, but not when it is aimed at other beings of Me. Your fight is to overcome the urge; to purge yourself of war and woe. None can hold to Me and proclaim victory over others of My parts as foe. *I am here and there; and everywhere. Justice is fair play with Me and Mine in My eternity of now.*

The "New Jerusalem"'referred to in the Bible,.

CHAPTER SEVEN   PRODIGAL MOTHER

in Rev. 21: 10, is not really new. It is the positive polarity "moon[50]" that has been orbiting around the Earth[10] for many thousands of years.

This satellite, called. "Shanchea[73]" by the space people, is a spacecraft. Their name for the Earth[10] is "Shan". "Chea" means child in their language of the Solex-Mal, or Solar Tongue. Therefore the name of this ship is "Earthchild" in Englih. This same craft was called the "Star of Bethlehem[74]"over nineteen hundred years ago at the bith of the child called Jesus.

This positive polarity spaceship is square. This is not new information. It has been before our eyes hundreds of years in print; though it was not recognized. Rev. 21: 16 tells you, "And the city lieth four[52]-square, and the length is as large as the breadth: and he measured the city with the reed, twelve thousands furlongs. The length and the breadth and the height of it are equal."

The reason it was called "The Star of Bethlehem[74]" was because when it is activated under control it looks like a star to physical vision. The last time its power units were activated was when the man man Jesus was born. This "Positive star body" generates a negative. force field around it to protect it when it is in motion as a ship.

"Beth" is used today as "Beta", meaning negative. "Le" is used today as "Lea", meaning a meadow. "Hem" can be understood by any woman as the thing that goes around the bottom of a dress. "Star of Beta-le-hem[74]" means a positive

CHAPTER SEVEN PRODIGAL MOTHER

body, with a negative force field around i!t, over a meadow. That is where Jesus was born in a manger, in a meadow.

Shanchea[73] is orbiting around the Earth[10] in the Earth's[10] positive force field. It cannot be seen by telescopes because it sets up no resistance to the Sun's[29] positive rays.

The Bible tells further, in Rev. 21: 11; "Having the glory of God[11]: and her lightt was like unto a stone most precious, even like jasper stone, *clear as a crystal.*"

The "Seven[1] Lights[66]" are spoken of in Rev.1:20;"The mystery of the *seven[1] stars* which thou sawest in my right hand (positive polarity), and the seven golden candlesticks. The *seven stars* are the angels[63] (space people) of the seven[1] churches (seven[1] levels of life around the Earth[10]) : and the seven[1] candlesticks which thou sawest are the seven[1] churches."

The population of this level of life on the Earth[10] is composed of people from the other six[71] levels. Chapters 2 and 3 of Revelations tells which of the levels you are from. One of these seven church descriptions fits every mortal in this level.

The population of Shanchea[73] is given in Rev. 5 :11; "And I beheld, and I heard the voice of many angels[63] round the throne and the beasts and the elders : and the number of them was *ten thousand times ten thousand,* and *thousands of thousands.*"

CHAPTER SEVEN PRODIGAL MOTHER

I am the voice, 0 mortal man, that whispers in the silence of your Being. I am the motion, instilled within the fluid dust of the body, to encase you in this density of three. I am the softness that all babes know when nestled to the breast of Me. I am the hardness of the substance many times beyond the density that mortals know. I am the sun that warms the morn', and scorches brow. For thou must know, within the Being of Me is thee. And search, though you may do for eons yet to come, I am not there where you may go. I am within you giving Life to clay, that My motion may be manifest for purposes misunderstood by man. I am not the formula of many, nor of one, My combination varies with each speck of dust, with each drop of rain, with each thought, each individual pain and hope. For I am always surrounding thee, and thee in Me but makes the journey short. Look not afar, look where you are eternity is Now.

0 man, you need not chart a roadway through the stars to Me. You need not cross the land, or search beyond the sea. You will find Me in the smile, in the look of someone you have helped along the way. You only have to search your heart and start to find that I am there wherever you may be. Though all the roads may lead to me; though many search eternally to find a shortcut in the way I am there and here, as close as you to Me. So reach no{ for a star afar, search not in the distance, in the future, or the past. At last you are aware that I am there within your Being, watching how you treat the Me in others of My parts.

CHAPTER EIGHT METHUSELAH'S TOY

CHAPTER EIGHT

METHUSELAH'S[75] TOY

The Great Pyramid ("Pyr" means Fire; "Mid", the equal distance between the extremes; PYRAMID: Fire, or positive light substance in the middle) of Gizeh, Egypt, is the only existant structure on the Earth[10] that remains intact after 25,816 years. It is the greatest power plant ever built on this planet. At the time of its use it could furnish more power than the generators at Niagara Falls could produce in a thousand years. The Geat Pyramid was never intended to be a tomb or a monument for the Pharaohs. Neither was it built by the Egyptians or Hyksos, as assumed by historians. It was erected by a remmant of the Adamic race[15] on this planet.

In order to produce the power required, the Pyramid was built in minute conformity to the measurements of our solar system. All dimensions were accurately computed to insure correct functional operation.

The Pyramid was designed by Enoch and built by Thothma[10] with the help of the true descendants of the Adamic race[15] (the space people) who had made a forced landing on Earth[10]. Knowing the <u>Universal Laws</u>[49] and their application they received timely warning and journeyed to Egypt before the sinking of the great continent Atlantis Enoch[77] and Thothma[76] flying in an aircraft called "vailx[78]". After landing in Egypt

CHAPTER EIGHT METHUSELAH'S TOY

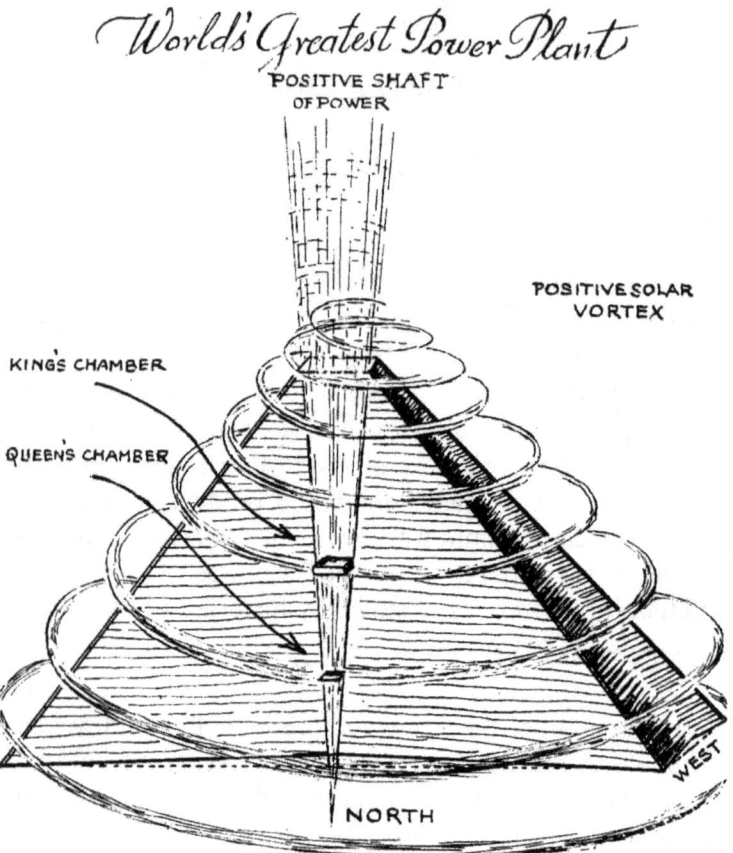

World's Greatest Power Plant

B— lines of force. They transported the heavy blocks with their vailx (a model T version of the spacecraft now in our atmosphere). Hovering over each block they encompassed it in their force field, eliminating the weight of the block in relation to the Earth. The blocks shaped so in completeness, as to assure astronomical precision, correspond to and contain all pertinent data of our Earth and Solar System. These correct dimensions were necessary in creating a positive solar vortex on a small scale — from the A^+ and B^- lines of light force.

CHAPTER EIGHT   METHUSELAH'S TOY

25,825 years ago, they started the operations and spent the next nine[79] years in building the Great Pyramid.

Utilizing knowledge gleaned from their secret records, they employed the infinite Light[66] powers. They knew how to manipulate the light[6] lines of force to cut the blocks with light[66] energy from the "A" positive and "B" negative lines of force. They transported the heavy blocks with their vailx[78]. Hovering over each block they encompassed it in their force field, eliminating the weight of the block in relation to the Earth[10]. The blocks shaped so as to assure astronomical precision, correspond to and contain all pertinent data of our Earth[10] and solar system. These correct dimensions were necessary in creating a positive solar vortex on a small scale from the "A" positive and "B" negative lines of light[66] force.

The Great Pyramid was erected at its present location for several reasons. Its location was on the side of the negative polarity from the Equator. The 30° latitude was the maximum vortex belt on both sides of the Equator. It was lateral through the Earth[10] to the positive pole of the planet's core. It was centrally located on the Earth's[10] landmass, which was its nearest maximum point of negative polarity. It was opposite to the Earth's[10] largest mass of water[48], which served as a reflector. The weight of the Pyramid had to be tremendous in order to prevent its twisting out of shape, or rotating on its base. The controversial capstone and a few courses of blocks were left off intentionally, as experiments proved they were not needed.

CHAPTER EIGHT   METHUSELAH'S TOY

As the Earth[10] rotated, each revolution brought the Pyramid intto a cycle of "A" positive and "B" negative lines of force. This caused an increase in the vortex-shaft of positive force (the principle of the cyclotron). Thus after a period of days the vortex reached and held its maximum force.

All this planning and work astronomy, mathematics and engineering was recorded symbolically in the stones as the work progressed. Jesus knew this by intuition and journeyed to Egypt to refresh his memory from the stone-records erected by his people.

In building this power plant of astounding dimensions their chief concern was the safe return to their own people. Being endowed with true perception, they visioned the coming cataclysms of the planet and planned an exodus. When the time of departure arrived, they entered the King's Chamber in the Pyramid and charged themselves in the super light-force vortex. Then they boarded their ships, hovering for a while over the truncated top of the Pyramid in the positive shaft of force which extended beyond the gravity range of the planet. When the ships were properly charged they were actually repelled from the planet and navigated with super speed to their destination.

Some of the sons of God (the Adamic race[15]), who remained on this planet, knew of and used the stored-up power of the Pyramid for several thousand years. For instance, Methuselah and his sons prolonged their life span for hundreds of years by charging their bodies in the vortex. Many of the deceased Pharaohs, placed in the "open tomb" of the King's Chamber for regeneration, were restored to life. Those who did not revive were left there for a period of 28 days[80], during which

CHAPTER EIGHT   METHUSELAH'S TOY

time the mummification took place.

However, as the Earth[10] moved in the Precession of the Equinox the regenerative and rejuvenating powers embodied in the Pyramid were lost. Rulers around the Earth[10], knowing of the rejuvenating powers of the pyramid, tried to duplicate the Great Pyramid of Gizeh by building a pyramid of their own by manual labor in order to live longer themselves. They did not fully know the principles of primary energy however, so their pyramids became their tombs. Nevertheless, the secrets are not completely lost.

Humans, knowing they are alive now, and not knowing what lies beyond the transition called death, attempt by every means possible to keep their physical bodies alive. The inner mind keeps transmitting the faint hope to their understanding that they can live forever. Naturally, knowing that they possess a physical vehicle now, they are reluctant to part with the old model to which they have become accustomed.

Monkey glands, hormones, operations, injections, etc., have been advanced by the technicians in biological and medical science to try to prolong the life of the physical body. People assume that substance of a physical or chemical nature can support substance of like physical nature. This is based on the theory that if you keep adding dirt to a hill that erosion is constantly dispersing, it will always be a hill. Nature always wins the battle in the long run, because natural forces are eternal. Man's efforts to overcome nature *by opposing it* will lose every time. The *only* means by which man can add years to the physical form is by *going with* the natural, eternal forces[60].

CHAPTER EIGHT   METHUSELAH'S TOY

Life is eternally continuous. Humans have placed the limits of *was, are,* and *will be* on life. These divisions of time are from the physical brain. The flesh we call the brain only *understands now,* it only exists in the physical body for *now.* It cannot understand anyithing beyond its own limits of birth and death[30]. All physical substance changes in time.

It is understandable when one has spent his years in building up associations, friends, and family, why he wishes to remain here longer. His brain concept of the physical body does not want to give up its encasing form.

The biggest trouble on this planet is, that when you get smart enough to do something with the knowledge you have acquired here, death intervenes. Our life span is just too short.

In Genesis, chapter 5, it tells of Seth, Enos, Jared[51], Methuselah[75], and others living for hundreds of years. They were so close to the knowledge of their ancestors of the Adamic colony[15] on Earth[10], that they used the "fountain of youth" principles to add to their lifespan.

Rejuvenation is done with the infinite light, or what is called "God power". In the application of this power the one receiving it does not see, feel, taste, smell; or hear anything. I have the information to make rejuvenation possible; adding 50 to 80 year onto the average lifespan *plus* resumption of youthful vitality.

The only difficulty I will have, is that we are on a planet that is revolving. In order to operate this apparatus I must clock it to the Earth's[10] rotation, quite like a large telescope is clocked

CHAPTER EIGHT   METHUSELAH'S TOY

to keep it centered on the object being viewed.

0 mortal beings, though many may express belief in the teachers I have sent, I accept them, providing that the expression of belief is not a living lie. And those who live My Laws and say "There is no God above", them I accept also. Though words may deny My person, the actions prove Me in the heart. Belief expressed in words is not verified in fact unless the living brings about the proof.

Though multitudes have closed the door that keeps Me from being the directing force, I condemn them not. Though Laws may make My Being infinite and boundless beyond comprehension, I am not there in the individual except as I am expressed in action.

0 mortals bound in density, look to the examples I have placed around you. Bow not your head to come to Me, only prepare that I may be recognized within your Being. Stumble not on barriers that mortal eyes fail to see. Build the perception within that may guide your path, that I may light the way so none shall stumble in progress of eternity. Lean not upon the cane of chance, but only cast a glance in My direction, which is within, to find the way by day or night. I make the path, I light the light. I lead you by the hand and yet you trust Me not, although you profess My Being in words. The cycle has come in the circulation of My doing, and now I lead My faithful ones to victory over self. For they shall recognize My Image is the light of sight, the light of right, instilled within each of My parts.

And though I shake the ashes of My universe., the furnaces of My heat shall ever be the Love of Me expressed in thee.

CHAPTER NINE   THE SWORD OF DAMOCLES

CHAPTER NINE

THE SWORD OF DAMOCLES[81]

I have explained that nearly everyone on this old Earth10 has the more or less dormant potential to communicate by thought. Like learning to play the piano, or learning to become a master of any trade, sport, or other activity, the use of thought communication can only be accomplished by regular, continuous practice.

The space people use instrumentation in their thought contacts with people, only to insure positive reception and to maintain power through conditions that could otherwise interrupt the reception.

They think into a device they call an "adiphon[82]". This receiver inturn transmits through a projector they call an "omnibeam". The "omnibeam" can be focused on any individual, or a group of people. This projecting of thoughts is mentioned throughout the Bible. Voices "coming from heaven". The "Lord" speaking unto Moses and many others, including the voice of God[11] coming to Jesus.

The space people have explained that they can only focus this beam safely on people who have devoted much time to an awareness of "open" perception. Otherwise, the beam can be dangerous to the physical health of anyone that cannot stand its powerful vibratory transmission.

CHAPTER NINE   THE SWORD OF DAMOCLES

One person has the power of one and can normally only contact one other individual. Here on the Earth[10] one power of thought is sufficient in the Earth's[10] magnetic field to contact any one other individual who is receptive at the time, anywhere on the Earth's[10] surface.

Thought projection by one person must be done by concentrating upon the individual you wish to receive your thought. Thinking his name, and what he looks like, must be pictured in the projector's mind several times. Then the thought you wish to transmit must be concentrated upon several times. This is for beginners. After one becomes adept at projection, only one thought, person, picture, in the projector's mind will be necessary.

The thought will not be projected rto the one of whom you are thinking until you release the thought. In other words, after the concentration you must immediately forget what you were projecting and think of anything else. As long as you hold the thought in your mind it will not reach the one you are projecting to.

Unless the person you are projecting to is in a receptive state, he may not receive the thought. To be receptive you must make your mind a blank. Do not think of anything while trying to receive the thoughts of others.

With continuous practice your projective and receptive ability will become apparent to you.

The power of thought can be increased by the increase in the number of people. One person has one power. Two people have eight power. Three people have 512 power. This power

CHAPTER NINE THE SWORD OF DAMOCLES

cubes its resultant to the maximum of twelve people.

This is the formula Jesus gave to the people when the Creative Spirit spoke through him, saying; "When *two or more* are gathered in My name there am I also".

This is the force that the <u>Supreme Intelligence</u>[11] used to think the universe[7] into being. Nothing can be manifested without first being[58] thought of by someone.

As I have said, three people have the projective force of 512 power. Four[52] people increase it to 134,-217,728 power. When twelve[83] people combine their thought force in unity, on *any* purpose, that purpose would be accomplished.

This is the reason Jesus did not select his disciples from among the intellectuals of his day. He would have had too many fixed ideas to undo in their minds. Instead, he picked common people from among the multitudes, only one of which could even write. He knew that it would be easier to use the power of twelve simple-minded people than to undo the dogma, custom, and religious illusions established in the minds of the "learned".

Most of the acts Jesus performed were done through the concentrated power of his twelve disciples, with Jesus controlling this tremendous power. These acts have been termed miracles by people who didn't understand them. *There are no miracles.* Everything comes aoout by the natural laws of cause and effect. Thought is the causal force of all effects.

CHAPTER NINE   THE SWORD OF DAMOCLES

Thought is of positive polarity predominance, as it is a causal, or projective force. In the physical level of negative polarity predominance, thought cannot manifest by itself.

Polarity requires that two poles be active to manifest a result. A battery with only a positive pole will not produce current. Duality is required in equal and opposite forces in order to manifest action as the resultant.

Motion can only be when unbalance exists. That which is in balance cannot move of itself. Some other force must cause the action. This is why the expression of "God[11] helps those that help themselves" is a universal law[60].

The Bible tells you that "God[11] rested on the seventh day." Nowhere does it tell you that God[11] started creating again. It says that God[11] completed His works. This means that God is still resting, and can only be manifested through man, who was given dominion over all things. This in itself is proof of reincarnation. God[11] made the race of man and then rested. Everyone of the race of man was created simultaneously. No one is older, or younger, than another. When God[11] rested, creation was terminated by God[11]. Birth of babies on the Earth is only the repetition of their eternal creation[16a] here, or somewhere else in the universe[7], before.

Death is only the departure from negative polarity manifestation to positive polarity manifestation. Life is only manifested through the <u>unbalanced opposites</u>[30,31].

CHAPTER NINE THE SWORD OF DAMOCLES

God[11] is nothing. If God[11] were a thing, God would have individuality and could not be infinite, for individuality is only a part of everything. God[11] is referred to as He, the Father, etc., by the church. This nullifies God's infinity and gives male gender to God[11]. This excludes everything feminine and of negative polarity. The church would have God[11] in the image of man, rather than man in the image of God[11].

To use God[11] power, you must bring it out of stillness and manifest It through expression, or motion, to produce a given result. In giving man dominion over all things except his fellow men, God[11] expected you to use the infinite Intelligence of universal Being[58] to manifest results.

Why did Jesus say he oame to bring the Word? He could have easily communicated with anyone he wanted to by thought, but he said he came to bring the *Word*.

The reason was that he knew the power of God[10] (Rest) could only be manifested in a predominately negative polarity level of life by an equal interchange of thought (positive polarity) and expression (negative polarity).

It is not my intention to prove this formula to you, but rather to let your reason and experiences prove it to yourself. Look back through your experiences and recall if the following has happened to you before. Apply it now and make it work now. God's[10] power has no limits except those that man creates. *Think* regularly every night between 6 P.M. And Midnight of

CHAPTER NINE   THE SWORD OF DAMOCLES

something you *need*. This is projecting positive thought, by concentration, into the negative polarity (receptive) lines of force, which alone are active in this quarter of the twenty-four hour rotation of the Earth[10].

Then during 'the time from 6 A.M to Noon, which is the positive quarter relative to the projective, positive polarity lines of force, express in *words* that you *do not want* the things you thought about during the 6 P.M. to Midnight quarter.

By attraction, positive thought to negative force and negative expression (the word) to positive force, you can receive that which you have put the forces of the universe in motion for.

This should be done regularly, night and morning, for 28 consecutive days (one magnetic month), and then release it by forgetting *entirely* about it.

This can be used for others, especially if you *do not tell* them what you are doing for them. Telling them will bring their mind action into play and will interfere with the results.

Once this formula is applied exactly *as* given nothing in the universe can prevent the results from manifesting.

You must *think* what you need or others *need,* and use "The Word" or the power of opposite polarity, and patiently wait for the result after forgetting about it or releasing it into God's hands.

The Creator[16] caused the universe to be. Then all was given unto the dominion of Man throughout the universe.

CHAPTER NINE THE SWORD OF DAMOCLES

Man, using the force of thought, can create new things for progression, or create new things for destruction. Thought is the prime force and is neutral.

Words are the effect of thoughts, whether they be good or bad. Words are in the range of our physical hearing. They are the means by which thoughts are conveyed between people with sound. Various languages convey the same meaning by different sounds.

There have been many arguments, discussions, and efforts to prove that things, and people, not seen in our life level, can be materialized. The Bible tells many times about "angels" appearing before people, apparently out of thin air.

To believe in the Bible of Christianity, with the concept that "angels" appeared in olden time, and cannot appear in our time; is certainly bullheaded orthodoxy. This is prilnarily done by some "Christians" who do no want "angels" to interfere with their selfish ways and pleasures.

Much has been said about thte space people of today materializing and dematerializing on several occasions. I can truthfully say that I have seen and talked with one of them that instantly disappeared to my vision; but I could still feel him when I touched where I had just seen him.

Just as orthodoxy places limits on people's thinking, *so* does your physical sense of sight place limits on your seeing. Your eye can only see within the range of the visible spectrum; about 4000. to 7800 Angstroms in wave length measurement

You cannot see the air; yet you breathe it. You can *see* water

CHAPTER NINE   THE SWORD OF DAMOCLES

in its fluid density and its vaporous density, but when the steam is absorbed in the air; you cannot see it.

Vibrations from about 20 to nearly 20,000 cycles a second can be heard with the ears. Vibrations below our hearing level are called "infrasonic[84]" and those above it "ultrasonic".

Because the five lower senses all have limits, people's thinking has become narrowed into a groove that will not allow them to accept anything that is not within their limitations.

Many of the space people live in frequencies of life beyond the human limits. By using methods developed by them, they can bring their body vibrations inside our visual limits as easily as we can condense unseen moisture out of the air into water,[48] and then freeze it into ice.

Many spiritualist mediums can materialize people from beyond the door of death. Do not let yourself to be confused, however, with these ectoplasmic[85] figures, or the words spoken through them. All figures of people generated through the ectoplasm[85] of another person are from the transition or Earthbound level, or are created from the mind of the medium.

This is not to be scoffed at, as the power to create from the mind is a great one indeed. *None* of the space people from other levels of life are ever materialized through a medium. It is not possible to bring through ectoplasmic[85] means, anyone from beyond the Earth's[10] force field.

CHAPTER NINE   THE SWORD OF DAMOCLES

In order to progress to the finer frequencies of life in other levels, you must first known where you stand in this level. The Creative Spirit so designed His light[66] universe[7] that nothing can exceed its individual vibratory qualifications.

Your individual record is being made daily by the way you live. Everything you think, say, or do is recorded in your aura. In the life following this one, you will only be able to progress to the highest level in which your light record will vibrate. No one is going to judge you but yourself, and you will be faced with the results of the record you established here.

You must conform in the way you live to the laws of the universe. The densities are established by different vibratory frequencies of light[66]. You can qualify to "jump grades" by the way you live here now.

I am the voice, 0 man, speaking in the stillness of your Being. The righteous recognize My voice. My call is to those whose ears are deaf to My withinness. I plead eternally, that all may hear the Me in you eventually. In the pattern of My doings I bring you pain and joy, that you may feel Me in the contrast of your senses. Never shall I cease to call to those who live in darkness. Though My patience is infinite, I suffer because of your sins. When you hear Me in another listen! Do not shy from Me in the disguise of raucous laughter. The ones who live in the clamor of confusion, to hide from Me, are only adding sorrow to tomorrow. So I make each tomorrow a today, that your memory of yesterday shall make My voice the louder from out of the silence of an added day you spent alone.

CHAPTER NINE   THE SWORD OF DAMOCLES

I have extended the Light to manifest My creations from thought of Me, and perpetuated motion throughout eternity. Each motion to bring an effect, and every effect a cause by repetition in an endless pattern of My doings.

I ended My work of bringing about, and made thee, 0 man, to carry continuity. My infinite watching is directed to see My Image of instrumentality, which is thee, 0 man.

Whenever you sing My heart sings too, through joy of your emotion. And when you assist another   the act of thee is devotion to Me, and from Me through thee.

Whenever you sorrow, I am sad too; each thrill you feel is transmitted to Me. I too am ignored when you fail to see the Me in others around you. Though you are effect of My cause, 0 man Intelligent Image of Me I only exist as effect of you whenever you cause Me to be an extension through thee. Then am I active, then do I live, when you give effect to My cause in the love of Me through each day of My days, eternally.

CHAPTER TEN THE FALSE CHARIOT

CHAPTER TEN

THE FALSE CHARIOT

You must understand that the substance you call your body is very much like the body of an automobile. The chassis on which the substance forms is the eternal part of you. You can lose a limb or smash the body and the chassis of your Reality continues on. In physical level requirements, your material body is of an animal structure following the form of eternal man in the essence of your real Self. This material structure is given life by the fact that the *forms of crystals* within the blood stream are the power house of your, every motion.

These microscopic crystals in the blood diffuse, refract, and reflect the positive-negative light passing through you continuously. These crystals often become neutral. They lost their power, like a magnet. Each of these crystals is polarized and carries polarity in opposition. This brings about the flow of your blood through light energy. Many .times as these crystals neutralize, they will settle in the feet. This is the reason for the ancient teachings concerning the position of standing on the head to circulate these crystals that have become neutral.

The heart is caused to function by the circulation of the blood, instead. of vice-versa. The heart serves only as a valve to keep the circulation going in one direction. The structure of arteries is such that the

cellular and atomic composition brings about a positive force upon the crystals in the blood stream. The

CHAPTER TEN   THE FALSE CHARIOT

veins are such that negative force of light energy functions through them. Being of animal structure, man in the physical body requires *crystals of an animal nature*. Various refractory crystals found in animal foods *are not reproduced by vegetation.*

The history of the mechanics of motion throughout the universe is looked in crystals. The records of all that is, all that was, and ever shall be are concealed in the frequencies of various elements known. and unknown in their crystal perfection. Life is only given motion through various particles of matter in many forms. As the Bible tells you "the blood is the life". It transmits and circulates light energy into substance form of animal nature, which conforms, to the pattern of man's real form. The flesh fills the real body, although the real body extends beyond the Skin boundari.es of the physical.

As you are born in this form, called the physical body, your instant beginning in this level was brought here in the seed, or the control master cell, through the infinite "G" line of light force. This control master cell was the beginning of your physical body. Under the functions of the control master cell, there :are many other master cells. These master cells compose each one a center, the beginning of your vital organs and glands. The brain is a gland. The control master cell is the essence of form. It is subject to absorption of characteristics from both the male and female parents. The consciousness of Being is the center of the control master cell, maintaining the records of !all previous lives and experiences in other levels.

AS these cells grow, bringing from a seed the form, controlled by the absorption of the control master cell, each child is endowed with good and bad traits of both parents.

CHAPTER TEN   THE FALSE CHARIOT

The seed which came over *the* infinite line of force contained none of the parent's characteristics.

As this control master cell gives instructions, each master cell comes to attention in the proper position in the body, like a well regimented army, all officers. Each of these officer master cells gathers recruits from the atomic substances in the "A" and "B" lines of force and develops each their own individual portion of the physical body. This continues until so-called "death" on this level.

Roughly every seven years these master cell intelligences, centering the organs and glands, are relieved by other officers. Roughly every 28 years, the control master cell is relieved by another; better qualified in more mature lines. The secret of long life is in the ability, through consciousness, to control the change of lthese control master cells.

Some people have assumed that the mind of individuals is in the head, because through progressive conditioning they have been led to believe that the brain iS the control of the mind. The mind is infinite and universal. The mind is not confined within the body.

In observing with the third eye, or the consciousness of your positive polarity vision, do not assume that the ability of this particular awareness is located anywhere within the physical body. Those whose concept of this vision is from the pineal gland area, will naturally seem to focus in that area. Actually your consciousness of individual being is all over your body, and in any particular experience *is* conentrated at the point of greatest sensation.

If you smash a toe and the toe hurts, that is the point at which

CHAPTER TEN THE FALSE CHARIOT

your greatest concentration of consciousness is recorded.

The consciousness of your individual being moves with your emotions. It flares with various ones of these emotions, and recedes with others.

Mind, being universal, is all through. you and you are in it. Your consciousness is the doorway to Universal Mind.

The scope of your consciousness can be increased with practice. Because you observe ahead of you with your negative polarity, physical vision, you assume to look ahead of you with your inner vision. This is limiting your scope.

A particular time to practice the expansion of your consciousness awareness is when you retire at night. When you close your eyes, do not attempt to concentrate a light, or your positive vision, at the center of the forehead. Attempt to penetrate into the blackness, into the depths, with your projective inner vision. Look into the darkness. Focus deeply and further away.

It is possible with practice to focus your inner vision as you do your physical vision. Attempt to extend your inner vision. Penetrate further and further each night into the darkness.

If you are outside observing the stars, try to look beyond the stars. In the spaces between them attempt to see another star where none can be seen with your limited physical vision. This practice with the physical vision will also expand the inner vision.

With constant and regular practice you should be able, within

CHAPTER TEN   THE FALSE CHARIOT

a six month's period, to throw the limits of your forward vision out. You should expand your inner vision to cover three hundred and sixty degrees and see as well behind as ahead, or to either side. The limits of your forward physical vision are not applicable to the inner vision.

The nightly practice will reveal to you that many things are within the scope of your inner vision, and your mind concept enlarges. Your consciousness penetrates with your attempt to extend your inner vision and you grasp more of what mind is.

What is life? What is light? Who is God? Where is heaven? These and many other questions are asked by numerous people daily. Wherer there is Life there is Light, and wherever there is Light there is God.

Orthodoxy preaches that God is male gender, saying He or Him. This implication gives to the Creator sex. The Single One is an "ity", composed of uncountable entities. The Creator is a power of Infinite; Boundless, Eternity. Wherever Life manifests motion, there is Soul in polarity opposition. Wherever Life manifests motion and consciousness, there is Spirit-Intelligence present as a part of the Creative Mind. Dimensional aspects of individuals in densities, leads to spiral inclinations of finer levels of life. You are all sitting in God, breathing God in, and He is manifesting Life in physical form through His right hand of positive polarity and His left hand of negative polarity. In-between the uncountable billions of lines of light energy passing through you, there *scientifically* is God; insulating the oppositely polarized light energies from each other. Centering your consciousness individually, there is the staff of Light and Life eternal.

Though God is still, the opposite light energies are in motion.

CHAPTER TEN   THE FALSE CHARIOT

When you move any muscle, light energy is the motive power. Light energy functions through the Spirit. The Single One is Universal Spirit unseen, potent, supreme Intelligence, composed of innumerable individual minds. When you record through any sense of smell, touch, taste, sight, hearing, thought, or Being, it is the spirit of you that records the action. The substance of flesh is inert to sensing. The conscious mind of God is yours to use, like a Universal library; but each must enter through his individual door to read the records.

Mundane philosophies, scientific theories, or religious beliefs do not serve as keys to enter God's house. You each . must individually open your own door and when you do, you will discover first that you were inside all the time, but were not aware of it.

Few people who attend church understand the beginning of the church. The church buildings today are patterned after an ancient worship.

Man and woman originally assumed they had reached a state of being part of God, in the ultimate in the physical body, when the woman gave birth to a child. The man and the woman considered
they had perfonned a creative act. This is the primary urge of all creation, to recreate. The understanding of the people was, that two things entered into the act of recreation. The male and female were
essential to birth.

In the time of the ancients, religious worship was conducted in the open. The ancient rites were conducted where a large rock pointed heavenward, symbolizing the projective male;

CHAPTER TEN   THE FALSE CHARIOT

and where another rock presented a cleavage, representing the female.

These phallic rites were conducted in reverence, although modem history would lead us to believe that they were sex orgies. The rites were worship in the most sincere form.

The church buildings today still present the spire to heaven as the symbol of the projective male. The double open doors still represent the cleavage, the receptive opening of the female.

Modern society does not understand sex and its relation to religion. *They cannot be separated.* The act of bringing a child to birth is not the part of the parent's choice. It is the choice of the child that brings it to birth through the parents. Although many would try to prevent having children, those who are qualified will have children in spite of themselves.

Throughout history, sex has been mentioned more than any other subject. The Bible is full of it. Everyone wants to be in on the act because it is the natural, conductive method of recreation.

Naturally, when any predominant thought is brought forth there is always opposition. Those who oppose the recreative act choose to isolate themselves and become ascetics. This is their choice, because primarily they do not feel responsible for bringing new life from the old.

Many of these socalled "masters" that have isolated themselves from society are fakes. They are escapists. They are looking for a way out of the responsibilities of life. They have no reverence toward anything, although they would present a "front" to make others believe that they are sacred

CHAPTER TEN   THE FALSE CHARIOT

people.

Throughout the universe, birth is a privilege of parents. It is the proof manifest that they are qualified to recreate with the Creator.

Recreation is the eternal progression of creation. Science is the art of measuring the ever-changing progression. The sciences converted to the destruction of today will only result in a disaster that will be a lesson for the future.

0 mortals cast in density of form, I center the Light to guide your way. My Light is not seen by those who observe only the density of figure. Neither can I violate the Laws I have made in the Wisdom of My eternal ways. I cannot but stay at rest with you, hoping that the best will reach for Me, that I may bring your perception into the Light.

Man closes doors, man hides himself. He binds himself to possessions of dust, not realizing all is lost to him and lost to Me. For only by the progression of thee, do I progress. My parts are scattered throughout My boundless Being. I move in any ways to fashion My completeness. Each part shall find the resurrection in Me, though the time 'is recorded in the records lost in space. My eternity is only complete in the patience of Myself in thee.

And so I wait within, with the knowing that My beginnings never end.

0 man, in the everchanging pattern of My thoughts I bring My creatures into being. In seeing motion al about, never doubt that I am there. For I am motion, change, and time, so that My rhyme of repetition may cycle all my parts.

CHAPTER TEN THE FALSE CHARIOT

Your eyes reach out to see the stars, not realizing each has stars within. Though sin may barricade your way to Me, change will be your sword to rend the veil and I shall hail you in your victory over self.

Though My time is naught to Me, time to you is meant to be a gauge to register progression in My ways.

Motion is the Me in thee, 0 man, to manifest a change, so that in time you may escape the rhyme of rebirth repetitions and be timelessly the peaceful thought of Me eternally.

NOTES

1 Seven corresponds to the seven days of the week, the seven planets, seven rungs of perfection, seven spheres or celestial stairs, the seven petals Of the rose, the seven heads of the naga of Angkor, the seven branches of the shaman's cosmic and sacrificial tree and so on.

Some groups of seven symbolize other groups of seven: thus the rose with its seven petals conjures up the Seven Heavens and the seven orders of angels, both perfect groupings. Seven denotes the fullness of the planetary and angelic orders, the fullness of the heavenly mansions, the fullness of the moral order and the fullness of energies and principles in the spiritual order. Seven was an Ancient Egyptian symbol of eternal life. It symbolizes the dynamic perfection of a complete cycle. Each phase of the Moon lasts for seven days and the four phases of the Moon (7 x 4) complete the cycle. In this context, Philo of Alexandria observed that the sum of the first seven digits (1 + 2+ 3+ 4 +5 +6 + 7) equals the same figure — 28. Seven conveys the meaning of a fresh start after a cycle has been completed and of positive regeneration.

Seven characterized the worship of Apollo and ceremonies in his honour were held on the seventh day of the month. In China, too, popular festivals were celebrated on the seventh day. Seven recurs in countless Ancient Greek traditions and legends — the seven Hesperides, the seven gates of Thebes, Niobe's seven sons and seven daughters, the seven strings of the lyre, the seven spheres and so on. There are seven emblems of the Buddha. The circumambulation of Mecca is completed in seven circuits.

SEVEN is seen in the hexagram (STAR OF DAVID). A week consists of six working days and one day of rest, representing the centre; the heavens contain (according to the old computation) six planets with the Sun as their centre; the hexagram has six sides, six angles or six star-arms, its centre acting as the seventh; the six directions of space have a mid-point or centre which gives the number seven. Seven symbolizes the fullness both of space and of time.

As the sum of the numbers Four (symbolizing Earth, with its four points of the compass) and THREE (symbolizing Heaven), SEVEN symbolizes the fullness of the universe in motion.

A group of seven comprises the fullness of moral life if the three theological virtues of Faith, Hope and Charity are added to the four cardinal virtues of Prudence, Temperance, Justice and Fortitude.

The seven colours of the rainbow and the seven notes of the diatonic scale

NOTES

display seven as the governor of vibration, that vibration which many primitive traditions hold to be the very essence of matter. Hippocrates is credited with stating that through its hidden properties the number seven
maintained all things in being, bestowed life and motion and that its influence extended to heavenly beings

Seven is the number of the completed cycle and of its renewal. Having created the world in stx days, God rested on the seventh day and made it holy. The sabbath is, therefore, not really a day of rest standing outside Creation, but its crowning achievement.

The Heavens are seven in number and so, according to Dante, are the planetary spheres. The Seven Heavens should also be identified with the seven notches in the Siberian axial tree, with the seven colours of the Buddha's staircase, the seven metals of the ladder in Mithraic mysteries and the seven rungs of the ladder of the Kadosh in Scottish Freemasonry, since seven is the number of the ascending order of spiritual levels which allow the individual to pass from Earth to Heaven.

At birth, the Buddha had measured the universe by taking seven steps to each of the four points of the compass. Four of the essential stages in his liberation correspond to the pauses, each of seven days, which he made under four different trees.

In folk stories and legends the number would seem to express the seven states of matter, the seven degrees of awareness and the seven stages of evolution: 1.awareness of the physical body: cravings satisfied simply and brutishly; 2. awareness of the emotions; impulses become more complex through feeling and imagination; 3. awareness of intellect; the individual classifies. arranges and reasons; 4. awareness of intuition; relationship with the unconscious becomes apparent; 5.awareness of spirituality: detachment from worldly things; 6.awareness of will; thought is transmitted into action; 7.awareness of life; directing action towards eternal life and salvation.

2 Light.(*See note #66*) In many instances the boundaries between light as a symbol and light as a metaphor remain ill-defined. Light is paired with darkness to symbolize the complementary or sequential qualities of an evolution. It's meaning is at all levels of human life, at every cosmic level a 'dark' period is followed by a 'light'.

Light follows darkness in the order of cosmic manifestation as in that of inward enlightenment. Their succession is as clearly observed by St Paul as it is by the Koran, the Rig-Veda, or by Taoist writers, or again by the Buddhist Anguttara-

NOTES

nikaya. It is another instance of Amaterasu coming out of the cavern. In more general terms, light and darkness constitute a universal duality expressed most clearly in that of YIN AND YANG. It is in any case a matter of indivisible correlatives, depicted by yin-yang, in which yin contains traces of yang and vice versa. In Zoroastrianism the opposition of light to darkness is that of Ormazd to Ahriman; in the West that of angels and devils; in India that of deva and asura; in China that of celestial and terrestrial influences. 'The Earth appoints the darkness, and the Heavens the light', Master Eckhart wrote. Once again in China, the conflict of chin—'ming is to be found in the motto of secret societies. Chin (to destroy) and 'ming (to re-create) do not carry the sole meaning of conflict between two dynastic principles, but re-creation of enlightenment through initiation. In Ismaili esotericism, the duality is also that of body and soul, symbols of the principles of light and darkness coexisting in the same individual.

Light manifests the forces of fertility released by the sky, just as water is often a manifestation of those same powers released by Earth. In countless central Asian myths, light 'is conjured up either as life-giving heat or as the force which penetrates a woman's womb'.

If sunlight is an emanation of celestial power, human hopes and fears do not regard it as an unchanging factor. It may quite easily vanish and with it life might disappear as well. Throughout human history there are records of a host of rituals inspired by solar eclipse and of daily human sacrifices to the Sun, their blood feeding its light. Among some pre-Columbian races, such as the Aztecs or the Chibcha in Colombia, these were on a massive scale, Here Sun-worship led to the growth of what were civilizations of fear.

Although the Sun may die each night it ts reborn each morning, and humanity links its fate with that of the Sun's light and derives from it hope in the continuity and power of life, for 'there is an essential kinship between mankind and the upper world'. Sunlight is human salvation and that is why the Ancient Egyptians sewed an amulet symbolizing the Sun to the wrappings of their mummies.

For example: The dove, embodying the Holy Spirit, which in Christian tradition came down to Our Lady, may be regarded as a revelation of the power of light. However, light may also be revealed as the ancestress whom the male impregnates rather than as the revelation of male powers of fertilization.

Light, for the Fathers of the early Christian Church , was a symbol of the Kingdom of Heaven and of Eternity. According to St Bernard, when the soul is separated from the body it will be 'plunged into a vast ocean of eternal light and of bright eternity.

NOTES

The symbolic meaning of light derives from a study of the natural world. Both Persia and Ancient Egypt, and indeed all mythologies, make light an attribute of the godhead. The Ancient World as a whole bears the same witness Plato, the Stoies, the Alexandrians, as well as the Gnostics. St Augustine was to pass on the Neoplatonist influence in praising the beauty of light. The Bible had already proclaimed its grandeur when it called the Word, Light of Lights.

Psychologists and psychoanalysts have noticed that 'ascension is linked to images of brightness accompanied by feelings of euphoria, while falling is linked to images of darkness, accompanied by feelings of fear. <u>These observations confirm that light symbolizes the maturing of the personality in harmony with the higher levels of being to which it rises, while darkness, blackness, would symbolize a state of anxiety and depression.</u>

[3]Symbolism: **Heavenly Council.** A meeting of God and His heavenly hosts. The concept of a heavenly council arose as a corollary to Israel's thoughts about the transcendence of God. They conceived of God as exalted above the world. God's dwelling place was in the heavens, not on the earth (Ecclesiastes 5:2). One prophet asserted that God sits "upon the circle of the earth" (Isaiah 40:22). There Yahweh presided over His heavenly council like some earthly king presiding over an assembly of his subjects.

God's heavenly council was made up of angelic servants often called "sons of God" (Job 1:6;Job 2:1). Micaiah saw the Lord sitting on His throne with "all the host of heaven" standing by to serve Him (1Kings 22:19). God sent these servants from the council from time to time to do His bidding (Job 1-2). Satan, the adversary, was among these "sons of God" in the prologue to Job. In his vision Isaiah entered the council and received a commission to preach to his people (Isaiah 6:1). The psalmist gave this insight into God's exalted being: "For who in the skies is comparable to the Lord? Who among the sons of the mighty is like the Lord, a God greatly feared in the council of the holy ones?" (Psalm 89:6-7). Eliphaz questioned Job's status with God: "Have you listened in the council of God?" (Job 15:8). For Jeremiah the sign of false prophets was that they had not "stood in the counsel of the Lord" (Jeremiah 23:18). Had they done so they would have proclaimed God's word to God's people (Jeremiah 23:22). The servants of the Lord in good standing are those who obey their Sovereign's will (Psalm 103:21;Psalm 148:1-6).

[4]**Universal mind** or universal consciousness is a metaphysical concept suggesting an underlying essence of all being and becoming in the universe. It

NOTES

includes the being and becoming that occurred in the universe prior to the arising of the concept of "Mind", a term that more appropriately refers to the organic, human, aspect of universal consciousness. It addresses inorganic being and becoming and the interactions that occur in that process without specific reference to the physical and chemical laws that try to describe those interactions. Those interactions have occurred, do occur, and continue to occur. Universal consciousness is the source, ground, basis, that underlies those interactions and the awareness and knowledge they imply.

[5]Metaphysical meaning of **Mind**: Mind--By the term Mind, it is means God:the Universal Principle, which includes all principles. The starting point of every act and thought and feeling; the common meeting ground of God and man.

The mind is the seat of perception of the things we see, hear, and feel. It is through the mind that we see the beauties of the earth and sky, of music, of art, in fact, of everything.

[6]**Superconsciousness** is heightened awareness. It is true wisdom involving intuition before reason and emotions. The superconsciousness is a state where "individuality itself seemed to dissolve and fade away into boundless being," which was "no nebulous ecstasy, but a state of transcendent wonder, associated with absolute clearness of mind."It is the awareness of oneself in perfect love, ineffable joy, and calm, expansive wisdom.

The superconscious mind rests above subconscious and conscious states. Whereas the subconscious induces dreams or sleep, superconsciousness does not involve the relaxation of energy downward in the body and mind. Rather, superconscious awareness uplifts the soul into a supremely peaceful and energetic state. The superconsciousness as the exact opposite of Freud's subconscious mind which makes man really man and not just a super-animal.

The superconscious state, also known as the higher Self, can be attained through meditation.

[7]**Universe**. Metaphysical meaning of universe-The total of all that is. It was first expressed as an idea in Divine Mind and later made manifest; that is, it became visible to the five senses by means of the creative power, the Word.

[8]**Parapsychology**: The study of the evidence for psychological phenomena, such as telepathy, clairvoyance and psychokinesis, that are inexplicable by science; the study of the evidence of mental awareness or influence of external

NOTES

objects without interaction from known physical means.

⁹ **One** is the symbol of homo erectus. Human beings are the only speies to walk upright and there are anthropologists who see in this their distinguishing characteristic, a characteristic more profound even than their powers of reasoning. One may be found in the images of the standing stone, the erect phallus.

One is also the immanent First Cause from which, nevertheless, all manifestation originates and to which, once its fleeting essence is exhausted, returns. It is the active principle: the creator. One is the symbolic place of being, the beginning and end of all things, the cosmic and ontological centre.

As well as being the symbol of Being, it is also the symbol of Revelation, the intercessor which raises mankind through knowledge to a higher plane of being. One is the mystic centre. too, from which the Spirit radiates like the Sun. There is justification for the distinction which Guénon draws between
one and Oneness. The latter is an expression of absolute being, incalculable, transcendent, the One God, while the former allows reproduction in its own likeness and reduction of the many to the one within a pattern of departure and return in which both external and internal pluralism have parts to play.

The unifying symbol would be charged with extremely powerful psychic energy. Jacques de la Rocheterie has observed its occurrence in dreams only when the process of individuation is well advanced. The subject is then able to draw on all the energy of the unifying symbol in order to achieve within him or herself harmony between consciousness and the unconscious, a dynamic balance of resolved contradictions and the cohabitation of irrational and rational, intellect and imagination, real and ideal and concrete and abstract. Totality is unified within the subject whose personality develops fully.

Symbolism: **God** as Oneness: In this book, Van Tassel followed the Judeo-Christian idea that God is One or the "Oneness of God". The Oneness of God refers to the "singleness" of God; that there is only one God and that there was no God before him or after him (Isaiah 43:10). Therefore, this singleness status of God never changes. The central teaching in Judaism, says that the Lord is one: "Hear, O Israel: The LORD our God, the LORD is one" (Deuteronomy 6:4). the Ten Commandments. It also begins with an emphasis of God as one: "You shall have no other gods before me" (Exodus 20:3). The origin of monotheism was not Deuteronomy 6:4, however. The opening words of the Bible are "In the beginning, God created the heavens and the earth" (Genesis 1:1). Only one God was before all things and created all things. This same one God was the One who spoke with Adam and Eve in the Garden of Eden

NOTES

(Genesis 2—3), saved the world through Noah (Genesis 6—8), and promised Abraham that all nations would be blessed through him (Genesis 12). Israel was always taught that the Lord God was the one God; the Jews were to reject all idols and deny all other gods.

[10]**Earth** Symbolically is contrasted with Heaven as the passive with the active principle; the female with the male aspect of manifestation; darkness with light; yin with yang: tamas (heaviness) with sattva (lightness density, fixity and concentration with rarity, mobility and dissipation.

Earth is the support, while Heaven is the cover. From Earth all beings receive their birth, for she is woman and MOTHER, but she is completely submissive to the active principle, Heaven. All female creatures share the nature of Earth. In a positive sense her qualities are those of gentleness, submissiveness and quiet and lasting firmness of purpose. To them should be added humility, derived etymologically from humus ('soil'), to which she bends and from which mankind was fashioned.

Mother earth (or mother nature) is symbolic of the environment from which life thrives. It's symbolic of nurture and growth and how the earth looks over us and provides life. It's a feminist symbol and earth is more naturally referred to as her/she in alignment with mother.

Earth is the "original producer", primal chaos, original matter, separated, according to Genesis, from the WATERS; brought to their surface by the hindu god Vishnu's wild soar; kneaded together by the heroes of Shinto; material from which the Creator, Nu-Kua to the Chinese, fashioned human beings.
The Earth is a virgin penetrated by hoe or PLOUGH, impregnated by water or by Blood, Heaven's semen. Universally, the Earth is a womb engendering springs of water, minerals and metals.

The Earth symbolizes motherhood — Mother Earth — giving life and receiving it back. Throwing himself on the ground, Job cries out: "naked I came out of my mother's womb, and naked shall I return thither" (Job 1: 21), identifying Mother Earth with the womb.

In Vedic religion, Earth also symbolizes the mother, fount of being and of life and protecting it against all the powers of annihilation. The Vedic funeral rituals included the recital of verses at the moment when the urn containing the ashes of the dead person was placed in the ground: *Creep away to this broad, vast earth, the mother that is kind and gentle Soft as wool to anyone who makes offerings; let her guard you from the lap of Destruction. Open up, earth; do not crush him .... Earth, wrap him up as*

NOTES

a mother wraps a son in the edge of her skirt.

The ancient cults of Mother Earth saw in this the fertilization of the mother, But the aim of the action is to bring forth the fruits of the field, and it is magical rather than sexual. Here the regression leads to a reactivation of the mother as the goal of desire, this time as a symbol not of sex but of the giver of nourishment.

[11]**God**. In Christianity and other monotheistic religions is the creator and ruler of the universe and source of all moral authority; the supreme being or ultimate reality. In other religions is a superhuman being or spirit worshiped as having power over nature or human fortunes; a deity, like the Sun God.

[12]**Infinite Being**- The quality characteristic of God.

[13]The word **religion** comes from the Latin and while there are a few different translations, the most prevalent roots take you back to the Latin word "Re-Ligare". "Ligare" means "to bind" or to "connect" Adding the "re" before "ligare" causes the word to mean "Re-Bind" or "Re-Connect. It is the belief in and worship of a superhuman controlling power, especially a personal God or gods.

[14]**Reincarnation**: The word reincarnation derives from a Latin term that literally means entering the flesh again. Reincarnation refers to the belief that an aspect of every human being (or all living beings in some cultures) continues to exist after death. Many cultures have found symbols of reincarnation in natural occuring phenomena like the the closing and reopening of the lotus petals symbolized the dead entering the underworld,and their reincarnation. Also, the frog is asymbol of reincarnation. Its form goes through a radical transformation: from frothy spawn containing myriad eggs, to the tadpole.

[15]**Adamic Race**: In the first ten and a half chapters of Genesis, God was dealing with man as the Adamic race. But after these chapters of the Bible, God shifted to another group of people. This second group of people is composed of the descendants of one father, Abraham.

Adam Whatever tradition and all its commentators may say — and a whole series of books would be needed to summarize their arguments — Adam still symbolizes the first man, made in the image of God. 'First' implies much more than mere priority in time: Adam is first in the natural order, he is the acme of

NOTES

earthly creation, the highest example of humankind. First, therefore, carries no trace of the primitive, the word bears no hint of the ape-man, planting a milestone in the upward evolutionary march of the species. He is first, too, in the sense that he is accountable to his long line of descendants. His primacy is of the moral, natural and ontological order: Adam is the pattern of mankind: he symbolizes something which lifts us to a level of study beyond that of mere history.

Furthermore, he was created in the image of God. From one symbolic aspect, the phrase may be taken to mean that, just as a masterpiece is in the image of the artist who created it, so Adam is in the image of God. Yet the specific point at which this masterpiece should resemble its Creator resides in succeeding where Deucalion failed, in making manifest the spirit within creation, by giving life to mere matter. What Adam symbolizes is the reality of the spirit — in the image of God, but other than God. From this flow all those other consequent innovations to the universe — conscience, reason, freedom, responsibility, independence — spiritual privileges, but of a spirit made fiesh and hence only in the image of God, and not identical with God.

Because Adam attempted to make himself identical with God, he also became the first to sin, with all the consequences that this primacy in sin entailed upon his descendants. In any order of events, the first is always, in some sense, the cause of whatever subsequently occurs within that order. Adam symbolizes Original Sin, perversion of the spirit, misuse of freedom and rejection of all dependence. Now this rejection of all dependence upon the Creator can only result in death, since that dependence is the very condition of life itself. Universally and traditionally whoever attempts to become God's equal falls under some terrible punishment.

[16]**Creator:** A person or thing that brings something into existence. A creator deity or creator god (often called the Creator) is a deity or god responsible for the creation of the Earth, world, and universe. Creation symbolizes the end of chaos through the introduction into the universe of a degree of shape, of order arid, or hierarchy. As a result, the Creator is the "one who eliminates chaos".

[16a]**Creation**: A creation myth (or cosmogonic myth) is a *symbolic narrative* of how the world began and how people first came to inhabit it. While in popular usage the term *myth* often refers to false or fanciful stories, members of cultures often ascribe varying degrees of truth to their creation myths. In the society in which it is told, a creation myth is usually regarded as conveying profound truths-metaphorically, symbolically, historically, or literally. They are

NOTES

commonly, although not always, considered cosmogonical myths– that is, they describe the ordering of the cosmos from a state of chaos or amorphousness.

Creation myths often share a number of features. They often are considered sacred accounts and can be found in nearly all known religious traditions. They are all stories with a plot and characters who are either deities, human-like figures, or animals, who often speak and transform easily. They are often set in a dim and nonspecific past that historian of religion Mircea Eliade termed *in illo tempore* ('at that time). Creation myths address questions deeply meaningful to the society that shares them, revealing their central worldview and the framework for the self-identity of the culture and individual in a universal context.

Creation myths develop in oral traditions and therefore typically have multiple versions; found throughout human culture, they are the most common form of myth.

[17]**Serpent**: The serpent, or snake, is one of the oldest and most widespread mythological symbols. The word is derived from Latin: *serpens*, a crawling animal or snake. Snakes have been associated with some of the oldest rituals known to mankind and represent dual expression of good and evil. In some cultures, snakes were fertility symbols. For example, the Hopi people of North America performed an annual snake dance to celebrate the union of Snake Youth (a Sky spirit) and Snake Girl (an Underworld spirit) and to renew the fertility of Nature. During the dance, live snakes were handled, and at the end of the dance the snakes were released into the fields to guarantee good crops. The snake dance is a prayer to the spirits of the clouds, the thunder and the lightning, that the rain may fall on the growing crops. In other cultures, snakes symbolized the umbilical cord, joining all humans to Mother Earth. The Great Goddess often had snakes as her familiars—sometimes twining around her sacred staff, as in ancient Crete—and they were worshiped as guardians of her mysteries of birth and regeneration.

Historically, serpents and snakes represent fertility or a creative life force. As snakes shed their skin through sloughing, they are symbols of rebirth, transformation, immortality, and healing.The ouroboros is a symbol of eternity and continual renewal of life. In some Abrahamic traditions, the serpent represents sexual desire. According to the Midrash, the serpent represents sexual passion. In Hinduism, Kundalini is a coiled serpent.

Serpents are represented as potent guardians of temples and other sacred spaces. This connection may be grounded in the observation that when threatened, some snakes (such as rattlesnakes or cobras) frequently hold and defend their ground, first resorting to threatening display and then fighting, rather than retreat. Thus, they are natural guardians of treasures or sacred sites which cannot easily be moved out of harm's way.

NOTES

At Angkor in Cambodia, numerous stone sculptures present hooded multi-headed nāgas as guardians of temples or other premises. A favorite motif of Angkorean sculptors from approximately the 12th century CE onward was that of the Buddha, sitting in the position of meditation, his weight supported by the coils of a multi-headed nāga that also uses its flared hood to shield him from above. This motif recalls the story of the Buddha and the serpent king Mucalinda: as the Buddha sat beneath a tree engrossed in meditation, Mucalinda came up from the roots of the tree to shield the Buddha from a tempest that was just beginning to arise.

In many myths, the chthonic serpent (sometimes a pair) lives in or is coiled around a Tree of Life situated in a divine garden. In the Genesis story of the Torah and biblical Old Testament, the tree of the knowledge of good and evil is situated in the Garden of Eden together with the tree of life and the serpent. In Greek mythology, Ladon coiled around the tree in the garden of the Hesperides protecting the golden apples.

The serpent, when forming a ring with its tail in its mouth, is a clear and widespread symbol of the "All-in-All", the totality of existence, infinity and the cyclic nature of the cosmos. The most well known version of this is the Aegypto-Greek ourobouros. It is believed to have been inspired by the Milky Way, as some ancient texts refer to a serpent of light residing in the heavens. The Ancient Egyptians associated it with Wadjet, one of their oldest deities, as well as another aspect, Hathor. In Norse mythology the World Serpent (or Midgard serpent) known as Jörmungandr encircled the world in the ocean's abyss biting its own tail.

In the Hebrew Bible the serpent in the Garden of Eden lured Eve with the promise of being like God, tempting her that despite God's warning, death would not be the result, that God was withholding knowledge from her. Although the serpent is identified as Satan in the Book of Revelation, in Genesis the serpent is portrayed merely as a deceptive creature or trickster, promoting as good what God had directly forbidden, and particularly cunning in its deception (Gen. 3:4–5 and 3:22).

The staff of Moses transformed into a snake and then back into a staff (Exodus 4:2–4). The Book of Numbers 21:6–9 provides an origin for an archaic copper serpent, Nehushtan, by associating it with Moses. This copper snake according to the Biblical text is put on a pole and used for healing. Book of Numbers 21:9 "And Moses made a snake of copper, and put it upon a pole, and it came to pass, that if a snake had bitten any man, when he beheld the snake of brass, he lived."

When the reformer King Hezekiah came to the throne of Judah in the late 8th century BCE, "He removed the high places, broke the sacred pillars, smashed the idols, and broke into pieces the copper snake that Moses had made: for unto those days the children of Israel did burn incense to it: and he called it

NOTES

Nehushtan. (2 Kings 18:4).

[18]**Spacecraft.** Symbolism: Spacecrafts as boats.-The boat is the symbol of voyacing, or of a crossing made either by the living or by the dead. Aside from the custom of exposing the dead in canoes, there are in Indonesia, and also, in part, in Melanesia, three important categories of magico-religious practice that involve the use (real or imaginary) of a ritual boat: (1) the boat for the expulsion of demons and sicknesses; (2) the boat in which the Indonesian shaman 'travels through the air' in search of the patient's soul; (3) the 'boat of the spirits', which carries the souls of the dead to the beyond. All civilizations have their boat of the dead. The belief that the dead accompany the Sun in "boats of the sun' is widespread throughout Oceania. In Ancient Egyptian art and literature the dead were described as sailing through the twelve regions of the Underworld in a sacred boat. It sails through dangers by the thousand, serpents, demons and evil spirits with long knives. As in the case of the weighing of the soul, its depiction contains constant hierarchical, ritual elements, enriched by occasional variations. In the centre of the picture the solar boat rides on the waves. Amid ships stands the Sun-god, Ra, the dead person kneeling in worship before him. At bow and stern Isis and Nephthys raise their left arms as if to point the way, while their right hands hold the crux ansara, the ANK, symbol of the eternal life which awaits the voyager.

The boat which bears the soul to this rebirth as a rediscovery of the cradle. It suggests similarities with the bosom and the womb, The first boat was perhaps the coffin. If Death were the first sailor, then the coffin, according to such a mythological hypothesis, would not be the last boat. It would be the first boat. Death would not be the last voyage. It would be the first voyage. For some deep dreamers it would be the first true voyage.

However, the boat of the dead arouses the awareness of sin, just as shipwreck suggests the idea of punishment: 'Charon's boat (In Greek mythology and Roman mythology,Charon or Kharon is the ferryman of Hades who carries souls of the newly deceased across the river Styx) always steers towards Hell. Nobody pilots the boat of happiness. Thus Charon's boat has become a symbol which will remain firmly connected with the immutable misfortune of mankind.

In Christian tradition the Church is the boat in which the faithful embark to overcome the perils of this world and the storms of the passions. In this context Noah's ark springs to mind as the prefiguration of the Church.

Symbolism: Boat as ship: Ships conjure up ideas of strength and safety in the dangers of a voyage and <u>the symbolism is as applicable to space-flight</u> as to sea-travel. The ship is like a star which orbits about its pole, the Earth, but under human control. It is a picture of life in which the individual must choose a goal

NOTES

and steer a course.

Here, one's found the following metaphor in the Van Tassel's text:

        Space   Spacecraft
        Sea   Boat

Boat ──────> Sea   (Discovering new lands, new worlds)
Spacecraft ──────> Space

For Van Tassel, space journey is like the journey of the ancient mariners discovering new lands. Also is the dawn of a new era or birth (emergence of a new humanity).

Symbolism: Spacecraft as a mother's womb. The womb protects the baby inside in the same way that the spacecraft protects the travelers from the empty space.

        Spacecraft   Travelers
        Cosmic Womb New Humanity

In this part, we have this Binary Opposition; As the Spacecraft is like a Cosmic Womb, the travelers are the forerunners of a new humaniy. The Cosmic Womb is a universal archetype that appears in the symbolism and mythologies of countless civilisations.

In Egypt, and subsequently in Rome, there was a ship-festival in honour of Isis which took place in March at the start of Spring. A freshly-built ship, inscribed with holy words and purified by blazing Torches, with white sails set and laden with perfumes and baskets of flowers, was launched into the sea and left for the winds to take it. It was intended to ensure fair winds and calm seas for the rest of the year. Isis' ship was a symbol of sacrifice to the gods to ensure the safety and protection of all other ships and stood for human society, passengers aboard the same ship of state or fate.

The old Scandinavian legend of the ghost-ship, on which Wagner based his Flying Dutchman, symbolizes the quest for fidelity in love and the ship-wreck of that ideal, exposed as nothing more than a phantom. In desperation the Dutchman wanders the seas, hoping to meet the woman who will be eternally faithful. Senta, for her part, emotionally absorbed by the same ideal, swears that she will be faithful to the Dutchman until death. However, in so doing she betrays her fiancé, Birk, and suffers the same damnation as the Dutchman whom she has tried to save. The Dutchman puts to sea, but his vessel founders, while

NOTES

Senta leaps from the rocks and is drowned. However, the pair are seen rising from the now-calmed waters, transfigured and redeemed by their sacrifice. Salvation is no impossibly idealistic dream, but exists in the courageous acceptance of reality. The ghost-ship symbolizes those dreams inspired by the highest ideals, but which are impossibly idealistic and cannot be realized.

Simbolism: Spacecraft as a mother's womb. The womb protects the baby inside in the same way that the spacecraft protects the travelers from the empty space.

[19]**Shiva**: Known as the The Auspicious One, also known as The Great God'). He is one of the principal deities of Hinduism, and the Supreme Being in Shaivism.

The figure of Shiva as we know him today is an amalgamation of various older non-Vedic and Vedic deities, including the Rigvedic storm god Rudra who may also have non-Vedic origins,into a single major deity.

Shiva is known as "The Destroyer" within the Trimurti, the triple deity of supreme divinity that includes Brahma and Vishnu. In the Shaivite tradition, Shiva is the Supreme Lord who creates, protects and transforms the universe.

Shiva is the primal Atman (soul, self) of the universe. There are many both benevolent and fearsome depictions of Shiva. In benevolent aspects, he is depicted as an omniscient Yogi who lives an ascetic life on Mount Kailash as well as a householder with wife Parvati and his two children, Ganesha and Kartikeya. In his fierce aspects, he is often depicted slaying demons. Shiva is also known as Adiyogi Shiva, regarded as the patron god of yoga, meditation and arts.

The iconographical attributes of Shiva are the serpent around his neck, the adorning crescent moon, the holy river Ganga flowing from his matted hair, the third eye on his forehead, the trishula or trident, as his weapon, and the damaru drum. He is usually worshipped in the aniconic form of lingam. Shiva is a pan-Hindu deity, revered widely by Hindus, in India, Nepal and Sri Lanka.

[20] Tree. Symbolism: The Cosmic Tree is a universal archetype that appears in the symbolism and mythologies of countless civilisations. It represents the Axis Mundi, or World Axis, that connects every aspect of the universe. From the giant Ash Yggdrasil, that connected the Nine Worlds of Norse mythology, to the Islamic 'Tree of Immortality', and the 'Tree of Knowledge' in the Garden of Eden, again and again the human condition is connected to the physical and transcendental universe through the image of a plant. The motif of a sacred tree is often associated with the figure of a serpent – an emblem of the shamanic experience, ascending from the shadows to the spiritual plane.

NOTES

This wall panel relief is filled with Assyrian symbolism, and at its center is depicted the Tree of Life or the Assyrian Sacred Tree. King Ashurnasirpal appears twice, dressed in ritual robes and holding the mace symbolizing his authority. The King stands in front of a Sacred Tree, possibly symbolizing life. Protective spirits are shown on either side behind the King. Wall panel, relief, Neo-Assyrian, North West Palace. British Museum.

Because its roots delve into the soil and its branches stretch up to the skies, the trees is universally regarded as a symbol of the relationships established between Heaven and Earth. In this sense trees possess the character of centres, to the degree that the World Tree is synonymous with the World axis. As axial figures, trees are therefore the upward path along which proceed those who pass from the visible to the invisible. This, then, is the tree, as suggestive of Jacob's Ladder as of the shaman's post in a Siberian yurt, of the centre-pole in a Voodoo shrine, or of that in a Sioux medicine-lodge round which the Sun-dance takes place. In Judeo-Christian tradition it is the central pillar which holds up temple or house and it is also the spinal column which supports the human body, the temple of the soul.

The Cosmic Tree is often depicted as an especially majestic species. This was the way in which Celts looked upon the oak, Germans the lime, Scandinavians the ash, Eastern Islam the olive and the peoples of Siberia the larch and birch. All are trees remarkable for their size, their longevity 'or, as in the case of the birch, for their gleaming whiteness. Pegs set in the trunk of the birch-tree marked out the stages of the shaman's ascension. Gods, spirits and souls took advantage of the World Tree as a path between Heaven and Earth. In China, this was true of the Kien Mu, a tree growing in the centre of the world, as the fact that it neither emitted an echo nor cast a shadow bears out. It had nine roots and

NOTES

nine branches through which it reached out to the nine springs where the dead dwelt and to the nine Heavens.

Some traditions hold to a plurality of World Trees. Thus the Goldi set one in Heaven, one on Earth and a third in the Kingdom of the Dead.

On the opposite side of the world to the land of the Goldi, in the cosmology of the Pueblo Indians, the great pine-tree in the Underworld shares the ascension symbolism of the transmigration of souls by providing the ladder up which the Ancestors were able to climb until they reached the light of our Sun.

The association of the Tree of Life with the manifestation of the godhead is reechoed in Christian tradition, since there is an analogy, or even a renewal of the symbol, between the tree in the Old Covenant, the Tree of Life in Genesis, and the Tree of the Cross, or Tree of the New Covenant, which renewed mankind. The Cross, standing on a mountain in the centre of the world, as wholly renewing the ancient symbol of the Cosmic or World Tree. In any case, Christian iconography provides constant examples of the leafy cross, or Tree Cross, where the gap between the upper branches reveals the symbolism of the fork and its graphic representation the letter Y, or Oneness and Duality. At the extreme limit, by metonomy Christ himself becomes the World Tree, the World Axis, the ladder, a comparison which Origen makes explicit.

Both in East and West the Tree of Life was often inverted. According to the Vedas, this inversion derived from a definite concept of the role played by sunshine and sunlight in the growth of living things. They drew life from above and tried to instil life below. Hence the inversion in which the roots were depicted as playing the part of branches and the branches of roots. Life came from Heaven and was instilled into Earth. There is nothing antiscientific about this concept, but in the East the upper atmosphere is sacralized and photogenesis explained as the power of heavenly beings. The Hindu symbolism of the inverted tree is expressed with particular clarity in the Bhagavad Gita (15: 1) and also bears the meaning of the roots as the principle of manifestation and the branches as the effloration of that manifestation. The tree rises above the plane of meditation which marks the lower limits of the inverted cosmic realm. It crosses the bounds of the manifest to enter those of meditation and supply the latter with inspiration.

The same notion is to be found in Jewish esotericism where the Zohar speaks of the Tree of Life as stretching from the upper to the lower regions and all of it lit by the Sun. In Islam, the Tree of Bliss is rooted in the highest Heaven and its branches stretch above and below the world.

In Icelandic and Finnish folklore the same tradition is firmly present. The Lapps

NOTES

annually sacrificed an ox in honour of their vegetation-god and at the same time a tree was set up close to the altar with its branches in the ground and its roots in the air

The medicine-men of some Australian Aboriginal tribes had a magic tree which they planted upside-down. Having soaked the roots in human blood they would then burn it.

In the Upanishads, the universe is an inverted tree, rooted in the Heavens and with branches which enfold the whole Earth. This this image might have a solar significance.

The tree as the source of life presupposes that the source of life is concentrated in that plant; and therefore that the human modality exists in a state of potentiality, in seed form.

The Tree of Life may originally have regarded as an image of the primordial hermaphrodite, but on the level of the phenomenal world the trunk rising to the skies, a symbol of pre-eminently solar strength and power, is really the phallus, the archetypal image of the Father.

Symbolism: *Mountain metaphor for Tree.*

21 Cain: Whatever historical interpretations may be made of the Old Testament story (Genesis 4: 1-24), they are in no sense affected by the symbolic meaning which may be drawn from the same material. In other words, to discern symbols in the actions charted in this chapter of Genesis, is not thereby to exclude the possibility that those actions actually occurred, it is merely to give them an extra dimension which takes them beyond time and place. And even if the events never took place in precisely the way described in the Old Testament, their symbolism endures.

According to the Book of Genesis itself, Cain was the first person to be born of man and woman; he was the first to till the land: he was the first whose sacrifice was rejected by God; he was the first murderer, and he was the first person to reveal the existence of death, for until he killed his brother, nobody had looked upon a corpse. Cain was the first 'wanderer' in search of fertile land and the first to build a town. He was also the man upon whom God 'set a mark... lest any finding him should kill him'. He was also the first person who 'went out from the presence of the Lord'.

The cycle of his life is of unparallelled greatness, since it is that of a man thrown upon his own resources, accepting all the risks of life and all the consequences

NOTES

of his own actions. Cain is the symbol of human responsibility. His name means 'possession', because his mother said 'I have gotten a man from the Lord', because he was the first human birth. However, the possession of which he dreamed was possession of the Earth and above all, Possession of his own self 'so as to possess all the rest. You have borne me in accordance with the will and with the help of God [he tells his mother]. Soon realized that he would not lift a finger to help me and that I had to rely upon myself alone. Remember this, you others, that the fire and the fury, the strength and the obstinacy for which you admire me, were things which had to win for myself".

To be truly lord of the work of his hands, he tried to crown God's Earth with the fruits of man's labour. 'I dreamed of reconciling God with his earth'. He tried to build a town which would show man's labours more clearly than the tilling of the soil. "I saw the city as another sort of ploughing, sowing and harvesting. What am I saying? It was to raise the Earth above itself, yes, to lift it upright in the image of man, by man who would in so doing establish his own kingship .... Its walls would have enclosed the space in which I expected nothing of him [God]'. The town serves as the prologue of the atheism to come.

But God would not accept the sacrifices of this tiller of the soil and planner of cities. Why? Cain could not agree to be 'least-loved by God'. He had been ready to accept any sacrifice 'if only he had offered the slightest sign of acceptance. An unlovely creature, I needed love more than anything else. With this it would have been easy to please him. Without it, I became the hardened criminal, when one look would have made me relent'.

Furthermore, God did not reward all his backbreaking toil. 'Let it be clearly understood," Cain said, "I didn't complain because Abel had all the advantages, but because I had none .. .. God remained indifferent to my exhaustion, blind to my sacrifice and deaf to my prayers". And so he rebelled. Not for himself alone, but for 'all of you'. For all of you who do not accept the mystery of predestination which divides the human race into the saved and the damned, for all of you who do not understand 'the scorn which God feels for earthly greatness, and the favour which he shows to the humble'. This was the divine order against which he rebelled when he slit 'God's favourite" Abel's throat with a sliver of flint. Yet perhaps the secret of Cain's attitude towards God lies in the fact that his offering was not complete. He held back a part of his labours, not realizing that that portion, too, was owed to God. Then, in jealousy of his brother, in pride in his own achievements, in rebellion against God, he committed murder and dispensed with God.

From henceforth he was doomed to wander towards a future which he had perpetually to create. 'We are going into the empty spaces of mankind which mankind in its countless numbers will inhabit. Our guide will be the ever-fresh

NOTES

dawning of the day. By never finding a resting place, we shall be everywhere. Our wanderings will measure out the world and at the same time build it up'. He goes on to find 'man's future free from Jehovah's presence'.

But he was forced to kill his brother, another aspect of his own self, and advance the hour of death. To gain his own freedom he was forced to resort to crime. Death 'is simply being forced to fall into a sleep from which there is no waking'. He thrust it cruelly under the eyes of the first mother. "That ancient bugbear, that lurking punishment, now you stand revealed! Under Abel's features we can see that you have the features of us all and that you reduce us all to the level of brutes' . Adam and Eve saw death as the final fruit of the Tree of the Knowledge of Good and Evil. Standing before Abel's corpse, Adam cried out 'Here and now we suck the juice of the fruit of knowledge, and more than ever it is bitter to the taste'. But he told Eve, 'We infected Abel's body with the germs of death'. Utterly rejecting this, Eve replied, 'What purpose then to pass on life! Oh! It is as if he had torn a hole in my side: my children will now go on killing one another until the end of time' . But Cain's wife, Temech, defended her husband: 'Let life be the winner, even at the price of death' .

It is true that death was bound to arrive, since it was the punishment of the sin of disobedience. Cain's real sin was that he 'anticipated Jehovah's plans. He added a fresh sin to the sin of which death was the punishment'. He brought death into the world.

[22]**Abel**, in the Old Testament, second son of Adam and Eve, who was slain by his older brother,Cain (Genesis 4:1–16). His name in Hebrew is composed of the same three consonants as a root meaning "breath" According to Genesis, Abel, a shepherd, offered the Lord the firstborn of his flock. The Lord respected Abel's sacrifice but did not respect that offered by Cain. In a jealous rage, Cain murdered Abel. Cain then became a fugitive because his brother's innocent blood put a curse on him .

The storyteller in Genesis assumes a world of conflicting values, and he makes the point that divine authority backs self-control and brotherhood but punishes jealousy and violence. Cain had not mastered sin (v. 7); he had let it master him. The narrator takes a somber look at the human condition, seeing a dangerous world of Cains and Abels. Nevertheless, God is on the side of the martyrs; he avenges their deaths in the ruin of the Cains. In the New Testament the blood of Abel is cited as an example of the vengeance of violated innocence (Matthew 23:35; Luke 11:51).

In Christianity, comparisons are sometimes made between the death of Abel and that of Jesus, the former thus seen as being the first martyr. In Matthew 23:35

NOTES

Jesus speaks of Abel as "righteous", and the Epistle to the Hebrews states that "The blood of sprinkling ... [speaks] better things than that of Abel" (Hebrews 12:24). The blood of Jesus is interpreted as bringing mercy; but that of Abel as demanding vengeance (hence the curse and mark).

Abel is invoked in the litany for the dying in the Roman Catholic Church, and his sacrifice is mentioned in the Canon of the Mass along with those of Abraham and Melchizedek. The Alexandrian Rite commemorates him with a feast day on December 28.

According to the Coptic Book of Adam and Eve[23], and the Syriac Cave of Treasures, Abel's body, after many days of mourning, was placed in the Cave of Treasures, before which Adam and Eve, and descendants, offered their prayers. In addition, the Sethite line of the Generations of Adam swear by Abel's blood to segregate themselves from the unrighteous.

In the Book of Enoch (22:7), regarded by most Christian and Jewish traditions as extra-biblical, the soul of Abel is described as having been appointed as the chief of martyrs, crying for vengeance, for the destruction of the seed of Cain[21]. This view is later repeated in the Testament of Abraham, where Abel[22] has been raised to the position as the judge of the souls.

23 Eve It is unnecessary to allude to the story of the creation of woman and her temptation by the serpent[17] in the Garden of Eden except to recall the essentials of the many significations for which she stands.

According to patristic tradition, Adam and Eve[23] before the Fall were clothed in the garment of incorruptibility, their baser appetites were governed by reason and, according to St Augustine, they had experiential knowledge of God, who had spoken and revealed himself to them. Free from all care, they could indulge in contemplation. Such bliss was to end with the Fall and the chief culprit was to be Eve, whose role was to tempt Adam.

What should be the meaning of Eve[23]? According to Genesis, she was extracted from Adam's side while he was sleeping: a sleep which St Augustine was to describe as being comparable with an ecstasy and from this arose the belief of woman's subordination to man. Eve was regarded as the first woman, the first wife and the mother of nations. On the spiritual plane she symbolizes the female element in the male, in the sense employed by Origen, that the inner man comprises soul and spirit since 'it is said that the spirit is male and the soul may be termed female' (Sermons 'on Genesis 4: 15). From their accord sprang their sons, as righteous thoughts and good intentions may be termed.

Eve signifies human sensitivity and the irrational clement in the individual.

NOTES

Given that only this part of the soul had succumbed to temptation, the consequences need not have been fatal. The Fall was caused by the consent of the spirit, in other words of Adam. Adam and Eve's quarrel, their falling out and Adam's placing of the blame upon Eve, arose from the enmity which henceforth divided soul and spirit. Man in his entire being sinned, since soul and spirit consented to sin. In this sin, the first step was taken by the soul (Eve) and ratified by the spirit (Adam). The Tempter (the SERPENT[17]) could not achieve his purpose by a direct attack upon the spirit, he had to employ the soul as intermediary

To relate the Fall to the inner spiritual plane is singularly enlightening; since to debase it to giving consent to sexual intercourse is to destroy all its 'meaning and significance. Such an attitude was not one which would be preserved by the early Fathers and by their commentators. More often than not Eve was to stand for woman, the flesh and lust, while Adam represented man and the spirit. This was not so much an error as a partial understanding of the myth of Adam and Eve.

When Tertullian exclaimed "Do you not know that you are Eve... and that God's judgement still lies upon your sex? (De cultu feminarum 1: 1), he was blinded by his hatred of women. The curses which the Fathers so often called down on women's heads were inspired by this entirely external and strictly literal interpretation of the facts. Hence a modern writer interestingly suggests that "Tradition has barely glanced at the topic of Eve as the female within the male, despite its current interest. It has often been regarded as a moral allegory of no interest to the theologian except as a substantial component of Augustinian and medieval anthropology.

Nevertheless there are examples of writers who accept this symbolism. Thus Plotinus retained the meaning of inner spirituality. It was exploited by St Ambrose (De Paradiso 2: 11) and made explicit by St Augustine himself in a striking passage in which he describes the act of knowing:

> *This act of knowing is like the creation of woman from man's side, of which the goal was to signify marriage. Each person should therefore strictly control that part which is in submission to him and become as it were conjugal within him so that the flesh does not work against the spirit but remains submissive to it... such being the work of perfect wisdom (De Genesi contra Manichaeos 2: 12, 16).*

The word 'conjugal' is the one which should hold our attention. If than's inner structure is 'conjugal' it predicates a marriage between two separate elements. It should be noted here that, when the train of argument followed by St Augustine in his discussion of the act of knowing forces him to display this conjunction

NOTES

and to define it, he compares it with the creation of Eve and with the marriage of the pair, Adam and Eve. Now, in Hebrew thought. as evidenced by the Old Testament, 'to know' carries the meaning of sexual intercourse, and thus Adam 'knew' Eve. In almost the same sense St. Ambrose had written 'Let none judge it misplaced to regard Adam and Eve as standing for soul and body' (In Lucam 4: 66). Hence the marriage of soul and body, of flesh and spirit on an inner plane, symbolizes the marriage of male and female. If the ends of marriage are the procreation of children, then the marriage of spirit and flesh brings with it a fitting end product, that of 'good works'.

Medieval writers were to be influenced by the Pauline division of Adam = Spirit, Eve = Flesh and the statement that 'Adam was not deceived, but the woman' (1 Timothy 2: 14). It was suggested the symbolism of Adam and Eve upon different levels, speaking not only of spirit and soul, but of intelligence and emotionality. of knowledge and of love.

Lastly it should not be forgotten that the name of this archetype of woman is a palindrome (a word, phrase, or sequence that reads the same backward as forward, e.g., madam or nurses run.). This is no accident. It symbolizes the fact that 'woman, like the ANGELS in Plotinus' theory of divine manifestation, unlike men, possess a double nature, creators of an intelligence and simultaneously its physical containers.

24 Tiger: Generally speaking, the tiger conjures up notions of strength and savagery, signs simply of the negative. As a hunting-creature, it is, in this respect, a symbol of the warrior caste. In Chinese geomancy and alchemy the tiger was set in opposition to the DRAGON; in the first instance it was a maleficent symbol, but in the second the tiger stood for an active principle, energy, in contrast with the 'moist', passive principle, lead as opposed to mercury, breath to semen.

The 'Five Tigers', symbols of protective strength, were the guardians of the four cardinal points and of the centre. There are several instances in Chinese history and legend of this name (*Wu ho* — Five Tigers) being given to groups of valiant warriors who defended the empire. Tigers are, espeally, animals of the north and of the Winter solstice, when they devour evil influences. That tigers are sometimes the steeds of the Immortals is because they themselves are endowed with longevity. In Buddhism, their strength is also a symbol of the power of faith and of the spirit struggling to make its way through the Forest of Sin, itself depicted as a BAMBOO-forest.

In Hindu iconography, Shiva's trophy is a tiger-skin. Natural energy, which does not bind Shiva and which he controls, is represented by the Shakti, who rides a

NOTES

tiger.

Tigers are monsters of darkness and the new Moon but are also figures in the higher world, 'the world of life and growing light'. They are often depicted as 'letting humanity, represented by a child, escape [their] jaws (the child being the ancestor of the tribe, likened to the new moon.

Malaysian healers have the power to change themselves into tigers, and it should not be forgotten that throughout southeast Asia the mythic Tiger-Ancestor is regarded as an initiatory master. It is he who takes neophytes into the jungle to initiate them, in fact to "kill" and 'revive' them.

In Siberia the Gilyak believed that "because of its habits and way of life, the tiger is really a human being who only takes on the appearance of a tiger temporarily'.

'The appearance in dreams of tigers causes an agonized awakening. It revives the terrors aroused by approaching the beast in the jungle or seeing it in zoos or circuses. It terrifies and fascinates by its beauty, savagery and swift movement.

A tiger in dreams stands for a whole family of urges which have become completely out of our control and are ever ready to take us off our guard and harrow us with their assaults. The powerful feline nature of the tiger embodies a group of instinctive impulses as unavoidable as they are dangerous. It is naturally more cunning and less short-sighted than the bull and just as untamed and even more savage than the wild dog. These instincts display their most aggressive aspects because they have become utterly inhuman by being repressed within the jungle. Despite this, the tiger fascinates through size and strength, although it may lack the lion's dignity. The tiger is a treacherous, unforgiving tyrant. To see a tiger stalking through one's dreams means that one is dangerously open to the animality of one's instinctual impulses.

The tiger symbolizes the drowning of consciousness in the unleashing of a flood of elemental desires. Nevertheless, if, as sometimes depicted, the tiger is fighting creatures belonging to a lower order, such as serpents, it stands for the higher consciousness; but if it is fighting an eagle or a lion, then it stands for the instincts attempting to slake their rage against the prohibitions imposed by that higher order. As always, the meaning of the symbol varies with the creatures depicted in conflict.

24a **Hu:** Wu Song, nicknamed "Pilgrim", is a fictional character in Water Margin, one of the Four Great Classical Novels of Chinese literature. He ranks 14th of the 36 Heavenly Spirits of the 108 Liangshan heroes. According to

NOTES

legend, Wu Song was a student of the archer Zhou Tong and he was known for his extraordinary martial arts skills, good looks and ability to hold a large amount of alcohol.

As a skilled fighter, one of Wu Song's feats was defeating a tiger in single combat. An independent and free spirit, Wu Song also had a strong sense of justice, where he would rescue citizens who needed help and avenge those who were taken advantage of or murdered.

Wu Song knocks a man unconscious at his hometown after getting into a fight when drunk. He goes on the run thinking that the man has died. When taking shelter in the residence of the nobleman Chai Jin, he comes to know Song Jiang, who is also fleeing the law after killing his mistress Yan Poxi. They becomesworn brothers.

Learning later that the man he hit is not dead, Wu Song decides to go home. On the way, he passes by an inn near Jingyang Ridge, which puts out a banner that reads "After Three Bowls, Do Not Cross the Ridge", and goes in for a break. The innkeeper explains that the inn's home-brewed wine is so strong that customers would get drunk after having three bowls and could not cross the ridge ahead. Still sober after three bowls, Wu Song demands for more. By the end of his meal, he has consumed 18 bowls of wine but still looks steady. He is about to leave when the innkeeper stops him and warns him about a fierce tiger on the ridge. Wu Song suspects that the man is hoaxing him to spend the night at his inn. Ignoring the advice, he continues his journey, armed with only a quarterstaff.

Near the ridge, Wu Song spots an official notice warning of a tiger ahead. Not to lose face, he could not turn back. As he moves on, he starts to feel the effect of the wine. So he takes a nap on a big rock. As he is falling asleep, the tiger leaps out from the woods, shocking him out of his stupour. After narrowly dodging the tiger's first three charges, Wu Song attempts to fight back but breaks his staff on a tree. Unarmed, he summons all his might and manages to pin the tiger face down with his arms. He then rains blows on its head using his bare fist. After punching the tiger unconscious, he picks up his broken staff and whacks the tiger till he is sure it is dead. Exhausted and fearing another tiger might appear, he then flees the spot after a short rest, and runs into some local hunters, who are amazed to learn of his incredible feat. Impressed, the local magistrate of the nearby Yanggu County (in present-day Liaocheng, Shandong) offers him the job of chief constable. Wu Song accepts it and settles down, and surprisingly runs into his long-separated brother Wu Dalang, who has also moved to Yanggu from Qinghe.

NOTES

25 Binary Opposition. Claude Levi-Strauss was a French anthropologist and ethnologist. He is often referred to as the 'father of modern anthropology'. He proposed (Binary Opposition Theory) the idea that all narratives must be driven forward by conflict caused by a chain of opposing forces such as a hero and villain . This is the way, according to him, how the narrative must function and binary oppositions are key into making a reader, audience, a whole society understand the differences between the two oppositions. They are only able to be identified against each other. Common Binary Oppositions: Good/ Evil; Dark /Light; Male/ Female; Loud /Silence Rain/Wind; Sun/Serene.

26 Symbolism of "God created suns". God as the creator of Heavenly Bodies, is at the same time Father of many sons (human family).

God	Suns
Father	Sons

1.

In this part, we have the Binary Opposition mentioned above. The hidden meaning of the world: God & Suns comes to light in this binary opposition as Father & Sons.

27 Adam.Symbolism: Name is derived from "earth" and can be thought of as representative of universal power. Body created from 8 directions: water - blood, stones - bones, sun - eye, earth - flesh, roots - ligaments, wind - spirit, clouds - thoughts, fire - warmth. Is the name giver to all things. Is the father of all kings, who become his direct descendants.

This is the Hebrew word for "man". It could be ultimately derived from the red soil from which he was made, the color red lies behind the Hebrew root adam [: 'a]. Word play between "Adam" and "ground" (adama [h'm'd}a]) is unmistakable.

According to Genesis in the Old Testament, Adam was created from the earth by God. He and Eve were supposedly the first humans, living happily in the Garden of Eden until they ate the forbidden fruit from the tree of knowledge of good and evil. As a result they were expelled from Eden to the lands to the east, where they gave birth the second generation, including Cain, Abel and Seth.

Adam was made a little lower than "angels" (or "God") at his creation and "crowned with glory and honor" (Psalm 8:5). (Rabbis speculated the glory of Adam's heel outshone the sun.) He was commissioned as a vassal king to rule over God's creation. The words "subdue, " "rule, " "under his feet" (Gen 1:28;

NOTES

Psalm 8:6) suggest kingship over nature but not over his fellow man.

As an English Christian name, Adam has been common since the Middle Ages, and it received a boost after the Protestant Reformation. A famous bearer was Scottish economist Adam Smith (1723-1790).

In this part, we have the following Binary Opposition:

Mother	Son
Earth	Adam

As a mother gives birth to a son, in the same way, Earth gives birth to Adam. The hidden meaning is that Adam was begotten through the copulation of Father Sun with Mother Earth.

28 Resurrection: Also called *anastasis* is the concept of coming back to life after death. In a number of religions (a dying-and-rising god) is a deity which dies and resurrects. Reincarnation is a similar process hypothesized by other religions, which involves the same person or deity coming back to live in a different body, rather than the same one.

It is is the clearest symbol of divine manifestation, since all traditions hold that the secret of life can belong to God alone. Apollo's son, Asclepios (Aesculapius) the god of healing, was taught the art of curing disease by the centaur Chiron. When he had progressed so far that he was able to restore the dead to life, Zeus, King of the Gods, struck him down with his thunderbolt. Such knowledge was forbidden.

There is a curious Lydian legend which, in one aspect, re-echoes the scene in the Garden of Eden by introducing a serpent which possessed the secret of life and was therefore able to raise the dead. One day a serpent bit Moria's brother, Tylos, on the face and he died instantly. Moria summoned a giant, Damasen, who crushed the serpent. The serpent's mate slithered swiftly to a neighbouring wood and returned with a herb which she laid on her mate's nostrils. He immediately came to life and the pair escaped. Moria, who had seen all this, used the herb to bring her brother back to life. In the present context, the legend is of interest because it shows that the secret of life is not in human hands. Only the serpent knew of the herb which restored to life, and thus it was that, in the Garden of Eden, it was a serpent, entwined around the tree of Life, which tempted Eve with the offer of some secret knowledge and led to our first parents being punished by loss of immortality.

In Mystery religions, and especially the Eleusinian Mysteries, as well as the Ancient Egyptians' funeral ceremonies, are all evidence of the lively human

NOTES

hope of resurrection. The rites of initiation into the major mysteries were symbols of the resurrection which the initiates expected, but they set the principle of that resurrection beyond human control. Resurrection, as myth, idea or fact, is a symbol of transcendence and of the absolute power over life which belongs to God alone.

29 Sun: The symbolism of the Sun, as multivalent as the reality of the Sun, itself provides a wealth of contradictions. When the Sun was not a god, for many peoples it was a manifestation of the godhead (celestial epiphany). It could also be conceived as the Supreme Deity's son or the rainbow's brother. Semang Pygmies, Fuegians and Bushmen regard it as the Supreme Deity's eye, Australian Aborigines as the Creator's son, kindly disposed to mankind. The Samoyed considered Sun and Moon as the two eyes of Num (the Heavens), the Sun being the good and the Moon the evil eye. The Sun may also be regarded as what makes fertile, yet at the same time as what 'burns up and kills.

In addition to giving life to things, the Sun's rays make them manifest, not simply by making them perceptible, but because the rays represent extension of the primeval dot and in so far as they measure space. The Sun's rays — to which Shiva's tresses are assimilated — were traditionally seven in number, corresponding to the six dimensions of space and to the extra-cosmic dimension, represented by the centre itself. This relationship between the Sun's rays and cosmic geometry is expressed in Pythagorean symbolism. It is also Blake's Ancient of Days, the Sun-god measuring Heaven and Earth with his compasses. Hindu writers attribute the beginnings of all things which exist to the Sun, the First Cause and end of all that is manifested, the one which nourishes (savitri).

It is true that under a different aspect the Sun is also the principle of drought - the opposite to the fecundating principle of rain — and the destroyer. Thus the Chinese believed that excessive heat from the Sun had to be destroyed by shooting arrows at it and sometimes — as for example in Cambodia — rain-making rituals involved the sacrifice of a solar animal. Cyclical creation and destruction make the Sun a symbol of Maya, mother of the differentiated universe and of cosmic Illusion. In another way, the cycle of the Sun symbolizes the alternation of life, death and rebirth, both in its daily manifestation (a universal symbol but one of especial richness in Vedic writings) as well as in its annual manifestation (see sotstice). The Sun is thus regarded as a symbol of resurrection and immortality. The Chinese Immortals fed upon the essence of the Sun as well as upon sunflower seeds, of which the relationship with the Sun is patent. The Sun is an aspect of the Tree of the World as well as of the Tree of Life, the former in any case being identified with the Sun's ray.

NOTES

The Sun is the centre of the Heavens, just as the heart is the centre of the body; but in this context it is a spiritual Sun which Vedic symbolism depicted as stationary at its zenith and which was also termed the Heart or Eye of the World. It was the abode of Purusha or of Brahma; it is ātman, the universal spirit. The Sun's ray which binds purusha to the individual corresponds to the subtle coronal artery of Yoga. It is reminiscent of the symbolism of thread and can not fail to conjure up that of the spider's web. As the heart of the world, the Sun is sometimes depicted in the centre of the Wheel of the Zodiac and is manifested in a similar way by the twelve Aditya. Although the universal symbol of the solar chariot is generally related to the Sun's diurnal transit, the chariot-wheel and Sarya's chariot had only one wheel — its itself pre-minently a symabol of the radiant sun.

If the light radiated by the Sun is intellectual knowledge, the Sun itself is the cosmic intellect, just as in the individual being the heart is the seat of the faculty of knowing. The name Heliopolis, Citadel or City of the Sun, was often given to the primal spiritual centre. It is the seat of the cyclical lawgiver Manu, Homer's Syria (Sarya, 'Sun'), lying beyond the island of Ortygia, an island 'where are the turning-places of the sun'. The pre-eminent Sun-god and god of initiation, Apollo, came from the Hyperborean world and his arrow was like a ray of sunlight. Similarly, the Sun is Vishnu's emblem, as well as that of the Buddha (some Chinese writers called him 'Golden Man' and "Sun-Buddha') and of Christ, too. His rays are the twelve Apostles and he was called Sol Justitiae (Sun of Justice), and Sol Invictus (Invincible Sun). Hesychius of Batos wrote that 'we look upon Jesus as the Sun shining Justice down', that is to say, as the spiritual Sun or heart of the world. Philotheus of Sinai calls him 'the Sun of Truth', reminiscent of the Transfiguration on Mount Tabor when Christ's face shone like the Sun. The Lawarum, Christ's monogram, is reminiscent of the solar wheel. To this one might add that the Jewish High Priest wore a golden disc on his chest, a symbol of the divine Sun.

Similarly, the Sun is a universal symbol of the monarch as the heart of an empire. Although the mother of the Han Emperor Wu may have given birth to him after dreaming that the Sun had entered her womb, this was not merely a symbol of fecundation, it was above all an imperial symbol.

The Rising Sun is not simply the Japanese national emblem, but the country's name (Nihon). The ancestor of the dynasties which ruled from Angkor was named Baladitya ('Rising Sun') and his activities are deliberately assimilated — as were those of the Chinese emperor in the Temple of Heaven — to a revolution of the Zodiac. Circumambulation always follows the Sun, wherever temples look to the East from which its daily transit begins.

The solar principle is represented by large numbers of animals, birds and plants

NOTES

(CHRYSANTHEMUM, LOTUS, SUNFLOWER: EAGLE, STAG, LION, to mention a very few) and by a metal, Gotp, which alchemists designated the Sun among metals.

The moon is always yin relative to the Sun's yang, since the latter's light shines directly while the Moon's is only a reflection of the Sun's. The latter is the active principle, the other, the passive. Symbolically, this has a very wide application, the Sun representing immediate, intuitive knowledge, the Moon rational and speculative knowledge acquired by reflection. Consequently Sun and Moon correspond, respectively, to spirit and soul (spiritus and anima) as well as to their respective seats, the heart and brain. They are essence and substance, form and matter. In the alchemical Emerald Table we read, 'his father is the Sun, his mother the Moon'. According to Shabistari, the Sun corresponds to the Prophet and the Moon to the wali, or the Imam, since the second receives light from the first.

In Japan and among the Montagnards of southern Vietnam, too, the Sun is feminine and the Moon is masculine — as, one is bound to observe, is the rule in German. This is because the female principle is regarded as the active principle, in so far as it is fecund, and among the Radhe, it was the Sun-goddess who impregnated, brooded and gave birth. This is also why, although the right eyes of such primeval heroes as Vaishvanara, Shiva, Pan-ku and Lao-kun are the Sun and their left the Moon, in the case of Izanagi the process is reversed. This correspondence between the eyes leads to another: the left eye corresponds to the future and the right to the past; thus the Sun corresponds to the powers of intellect and the Moon to those of memory.

The duality of Sun and Moon is also that of Vishnu and Shiva. There is an echo of this in the solar and lunar dynasties of India, Cambodia and Champa. The marriage of Sun and Moon is Harihara, part- Vishnu and part-Shiva, a favourite symbol in pre-Angkorian art. In Chinese it is also light (ming), its character composed of a synthesis of those denoting Sun and Moon .

In Central American tradition solar symbolism contrasts with lunar in another aspect. 'Sunset is not recognized as a "death" (unlike the moon's three days in hiding) but as a descent into the lower regions, into the kingdom of the dead. Unlike the moon, the sun has the privilege of passing through hell without undergoing the condition of death'. Hence the genuinely solar properties of the eagle among shamanistic attributes.

The opposition of Sun and Moon generally overlays male-female dualism. According to ancient tradition, at Teotihuacan, men were sacrificed to the Sun and women to the Moon. The Ancient Mexicans believed that we live under a fifth Sun. The four earlier Suns were those successively of the tiger, of wind, of

NOTES

rain (or fire) and of water. The first was that of Tezcatlipoca, linked to cold, to darkness and to the north; the second, of Quetzalcoatt in his original shape, linked to witchcraft and the west; the third, of the rain-god Tlaloc, linked to the south; the fourth, of the water-goddess Calchiuhtlicue, linked to the east.

Our Sun, the fifth, was placed beneath the sign of one of the fire-gods, Xiuhtecuhtli, sometimes depicted as a butterfly. All these ages, which they called Suns, ended in cataclysms when the four tigers devoured mankind, the four winds blew them away and the four rains and the four waters drowned them. The present age will be brought to an end by four earthquakes, and that will be the finish of the fifth Sun.

The great god of the midday Sun in the Aztec pantheon, Huitzilopochtli,was depicted as an eagle holding a starry serpent in its beak.

What most strikingly epitomize the basic symbolic dualism founded upon the pairing of Sun and Moon are the attributes of exogamic division among the Omaha Indians. This was given physical expression in the way in which, in their encampments, their tents were separated into two semicircles. The first presided over all religious activities associated with the Sun, the day, the north, the higher, the male principle and the right side, the second over the duties of politics and society, associated with the Moon, the night, the lower, the female principle and the left side.

In most nomadic pastoral societies the Sun is female (Mother Sun) and the Moon male (Father Moon): this is true of most of the Mongol and Turkic peoples of central Asia.

In Celtic, as in all ancient Indo-European languages, the noun, Sun, is feminine. In myth it was personified by Lug ('Light') who was called 'grianainech, 'Sun-face'. The same epithet is applied, either by analogy or extension, to the war-god, Ogma, who by definition possessed or ruled the dark side of the world. The Sun was, however, regarded above all as one of the basic elements in the universe. It was the most important among those (Moon, water, air and so on) called upon to witness a formal oath.

In astrology, the Sun is the symbol of life, heat, day, light, authority, the male sex and all things radiant. If astrologers seem to have lowered it to the, level of a mere PLANET, to be compared with a Mars or a Jupiter, this is chiefly because its influence is, so to speak, divided into two quite separate fields, one of direct influence through its position in the Heavens and the other indirect, being that of the zopiac. In fact all influence exerted by the signs of the Zodiac is essentially solar, being, in actual fact, the influence of the Sun reflected or polarized by the Earth's orbit.

NOTES

In its role of cosmic symbol, the Sun ranks as a true astral religion, its worship dominating the great civilizations of antiquity with their gigantic figures of gods and heroes — Atum, Osiris, Baal, Mithras, Helios, Apollo and so on — embodying the powers of creation and the sources of light and life represented by the Sun. Peoples with astral mythologies regard the Sun as a father-symbol, something reflected in children's drawings and in dreams. In the same way, the Sun has always been the astrologers' symbol of the male principle of generation and of the principle of authority of which the father is the individual's earliest embodiment. This is also true of that area of the psyche created by paternal influence in the form of training, education, awareness, discipline and morality. Thus, in a horoscope the Sun stands for Durkheim's social constraint and Freud's 'censorship' and is the source of social drives, civilization, ethics and all major aspects of existence. Its range of properties stretches from the negative super-ego which crushes the individual with taboos, principles, rules or prejudices, to the positive, idealized ego, a higher image of self to which the individual attempts to lift him-or herself. The day-star therefore locates the individual within a life which may be strictly regulated or highly sublimated: it represents the outlook offered by his personality through psychic syntheses, at the highest level, of the greatest demands, the loftiest aspirations and the strongest forms of individuation, or else in the total failure of pride or power-madness. It stands for the individual achieving the goals of marriage and parenthood, in worldly success which is an extension of his or her personal qualities, and in the very fact that he has achieved success by embodying the powers and authority inherent in the ultimate solarization of guide, leader, hero and ruler.

The Sun as giver of light and the Heavens which it illuminates as symbolizing the intellect and the superconsciousness. The intellect corresponds to consciousness and the spirit to superconsciousness. Thus the Sun and its rays, which were once symbols of fecundation, have become symbols of enlightenment. This is the key which enables psychoanalysis to unlock the meaning of all myths which show Sun-gods or solar heroes in action.

The Black Sun is the Sun in its nightly transit, when it leaves this world to shed its light upon another. The Aztecs depicted the Black Sun carried 'on the back of the god of the Underworld. It is the antithesis of the midday Sun, as the maleficent and destroying absolute of death. The Mayas depicted the Black Sun as a JAGUAR. Alchemists saw the Black Sun as unworked, primal matter, still to be set on the path of development. To the psychoanalyst, the Black Sun stands for the unconscious, again in its most elemental form. Traditionally the Black Sun presages the unleashing of destructive forces upon the universe, society or the individual. It heralds disaster, suffering, and death, the inverted image of the noonday Sun, hence the universal sense of ill omen attaching to eclipses.

NOTES

[30]**Binary Opposition: Light/Darkness.** Derived from the text, one made the following table:

Light	Darkness
Good	Evil

The table above can reveal the hidden symbolism behind the dyad Light/Darkness. One term dominated over the other. Once identified, this can elucidate the hidden symbolism encoded in the text. By examining this pattern of oppositions, it can show the deeper meaning in these dyads. Light is to Good, as Darkness is to Evil. In the long run, Light will overcome Darkness, and a second Garden of Eden will emerge.

[31] **Binary Opposition:**

Positive	Negative
Male	Female

This is the notion that prevails in the Bible with a misogynistic God

Female → Negative
Man → Positive

[32] **Law of action and reaction** is the third law of Newton's laws of motion. It is also commonly called as Newton's third law. This law simply states that: whenever a body exerts a force on a second body, the second body will exert an equal force in magnitude and opposite direction.

[33] From a metaphysical viewpoint, the physical world that we see before us is the 3rd dimension. There are other physical dimensions ranging from the 1st to the 7th dimensions. However, these dimensions are not so much physical dimensions but dimensions of Consciousness.

Third density is the density of self-awareness and the first density of consciousness of the spirit. It is the "axis upon which the creation turns" because in it entities choose the way (either service to others or service to self) in which they will further their evolution toward the Creator. Third density is much shorter than the other densities, taking only 75,000 years.

[34]**Fouth density.** The Fourth density is the density of love or understanding. Those who have successfully chosen a path come together with

NOTES

others of like mind in what has been called a "social memory complex" in order to pursue that path, either loving self or loving others . Fourth density lasts approximately 30 million years; fourth-density lifespans are approximately 90 thousand years.

[35]**Golden Rule**. The Golden Rule is the principle of treating others as one wants to be treated. It is a maxim that is found in most religions and cultures. It can be considered an ethic of reciprocity in some religions, although different religions treat it differently.

[36]**Vela Sector**. The Vela constellation lies in the southern hemisphere. Its name means "the sails" in Latin. The constellation represents the sails of the Argo Navis, the ship on which Jason and the Argonauts sailed on their quest for the Golden Fleece. It was once part of the much larger constellation Argo Navis, which was divided into three smaller constellations – Vela (the sails), Carina (the keel) and Puppi (the stern) – by the French astronomer Nicolas Louis de Lacaille in the 1750s.

Argo Navis was one of the 48 Greek constellations, first catalogued by the Greek astronomer Claudius Ptolemy in the 2nd century CE.

Vela contains a number of interesting stars and deep sky objects, among them the Eight-Burst Nebula (NGC 3132), the Gum Nebula, the Vela Supernova Remnant, the Pencil Nebula (NGC 2736), and the Omicron Velorum Cluster (IC 2391).

Vela is the 32nd constellation in size, occupying an area of 500 square degrees. It is located in the second quadrant of the southern hemisphere (SQ2) and can be seen at latitudes between +30° and -90°. The neighboring constellations are Antlia, Carina, Centaurus, Puppi and Pyxis.

Vela belongs to the Heavenly Waters family of constellations, along with Carina, Columba, Delphinus, Equuleus, Eridanus, Piscis Austrinus, Puppis and Pyxis.

Vela contains seven stars with known planets and has no Messier objects. The brightest star in the constellation is Gamma Velorum, with an apparent magnitude of 1.75. There are three meteor showers associated with the constellation: the Delta Velids, the Gamma Velids, and the Puppid-Velids.

NOTES

37Magnetic Pole Reversal or **geomagnetic reversal** is a change in a planet's magnetic field such that the positions of magnetic north and magnetic south are interchanged (not to be confused with geographic north and geographic south). The Earth's field has alternated between periods of normal polarity, in which the predominant direction of the field was the same as the present direction, and reverse polarity, in which it was the opposite. These periods are called chrons.

Reversal occurrences are statistically random. There have been 183 reversals over the last 83 million years (on average once every 450,000 years). The latest, the Brunhes–Matuyama reversal, occurred 780,000 years ago, with widely varying estimates of how quickly it happened. Other sources estimate that the time that it takes for a reversal to complete is on average around 7000 years for the four most recent reversals. This duration is dependent on latitude, with shorter durations at low latitudes, and longer durations at mid and high latitudes. Although variable, the duration of a full reversal is typically between 2000 and 12000 years.

38 First density is the density of awareness, in which the planet moves out of the timeless state into physical manifestation. Its elements are earth, air, water, and fire. On earth, after matter had coalesced and space/time had begun to "unroll its scroll of livingness", first density took about two billion years.

39Ark is like a Basket. There are various aspects to the symbolism of the ark and of voyaging in general which are linked together. The best known of these is Noah's Ark which sailed on the waters of the Flood, freighted with everything needed to restore the natural cycle. Sanskrit Puranic literature contains a similar account of how Manu, lawgiver to the present cycle, took ship with the Vedas, which are the seeds of the cyclic manifestation, and was saved by the Matsaya-avatara, the god Vishnu in his incarnation as a fish. In fact the Ark floated 'on the face of the waters', exactly like the World Egg — 'like the first seed of life', St Martin writes. The same symbol of the 'seed', the unspoken worp, which will germinate in some future cycle, recurs in the concH and in the Arabic letter min (a semicircle, the 'ark', with a dot, the 'seed', in the middle). It has drawn attention to the importance of the way in which the Rainbow complements the Ark by appearing over it as a sign of the 'covenant'. We have here two analogous but opposing symbols — one relative to 'the waters under the earth' and the other to the waters above it — which complement one another to recreate the ring of the unified cycle.

The symbolism of the Ark of the Covenant of the Children of Israel is closer

NOTES

than might be thought to the foregoing. The Israelites set it in the furthest end of the Tabernacle. It held the two tables of the Law, Aaron's Rod and a pot full of the manna on which the people were fed in the wilderness. It was the pledge of God's protection and the Israelites took it with them on their military campaigns. When it was translated with due ceremony to David's palace. the oxen pulling the cart stumbled, the Ark slipped and the man who put out his hand to steady it was instantly struck dead. You do not lightly touch what is holy, divine or tradition (2 Samuel 16).

The Ark contained the essence of tradition, but developed in the form of the Tables of the Law. According to St Martin it is 'the source of the Powers' of the cycle. Furthermore, a legend claims that it was hidden by Jeremiah on his return from the captivity in Babylon and that it will come to light again to usher in a new age.

In Christian tradition the Ark was one of the richest sources of symbolism. Noah's Ark stood as the symbol of the house protected by God preserving all living things. The Ark of the Covenant was the symbol of God's presence among his chosen people, a portable sanctuary, the pledge of the covenant between God and his people, and, finally, it was the symbol of the Church. It is clad in the triple symbolic meaning of the New Covenant, which is universal and eternal; of the new presence, which is 'real', and of the new ark of salvation. no longer from the Flood but from sin. It is the Church. the new Ark. available to all for the salvation of the world.

Noah's Ark has been the subject of much speculation, especially among Rabbinical writers. Its pyramidal form conveys a sense of fire or flame. It holds a phallic power. The Ark was built from the immortal wood, Mer, which is not subject to decay (a pine or acacia). There is a close connection between the dimensions God ordained for Noah's Ark at the time of the Flood and those which were given to Moses for the building of the Ark of the Covenant, the latter being proportionate with the former but on a much smaller scale. Noah's Ark had three decks. The importance of that figure is inescapable: it is a symbol of spiritual ascent.

Origen explains the dimensions of Noah's Ark: its length of 300 cubits expresses simultaneously the number one hundred and the number three: the first signifies the fullness of unity, the second the Trinity. Its breadth of fifty cubits is interpreted as the symbol of the Redemption. As to its height, it symbolizes the number one, by reason of the unity of God. Origen offers further analogies between the length, breadth and height of the Ark and the length, breadth and depth of the love of God of which St Paul speaks (Ephesians 3: 18). To St Ambrose the Ark also represented the human body in its dimensions and properties, while Isidore of Seville was to point out that 300 cubits equals six

NOTES

times fifty, thus the length is stx times the breadth and symbolizes the six ages of the world. St Augustine comments on this topic of the Ark that it prefigures the City of God. the Church and Christ's body.

In his treatise De arca Noe morali et de arca mystica, Hugh of St Victor takes up Origen's grand ideas once more. The mystic Ark is represented in the human heart. Hugh also compares it with a ship. He scrutinizes in succession the different components of the Ark to give a threefold interpretation of it, literal, moral and allegorical.

The Ark of the Heart is analogous with that most secret place within the Temple where sacrifice was offered, that is to say with the Holy of Holies. The Ark always retains a mysterious character. Jung finds the image of the mother's breast in it, the sea into which the Sun is swallowed. only to rise again. It is also the alchemical still in which base metals are transmuted. It is also the Holy Grail The heart as an ark or a still is a persistent symbol. Man's heart is the vessel in which the human is transmuted into the divine.

The Ark is a symbol of the treasure chest, the treasure being knowledge and life. It is the principle of individual preservation and resurrection. In Sudanese legend Nommo sends the first blacksmith to mankind. He comes down the rainbow bearing an Ark containing one example of every living thing, of each of the minerals and of all the crafts.

[40]**Solar boats** were the vessels used by the sun god Ra in ancient Egyptian mythology. During the day, Ra was said to use a vessel called the *Mandjet* or the Boat of Millions of Years, and the vessel he used during the night was known as the *Mesektet*. Ra was said to travel through the sky on the barge, providing light to the world. Each twelfth of his journey formed one of the twelve Egyptian hours of the day, each overseen by a protective deity. Ra then rode the barque through the underworld, with each hour of the night considered a gate overseen by twelve more protective deities. Passing through all of these while fending off various destructive monsters, Ra reappeared each day on the eastern horizon. He was said to travel across the sky in the *Mandjet* Boat through the hours of the day, and then switch to the *Mesektet* Boat to descend into the underworld for the hours of the night.

[41]**Spiral**. The spiral, a frequent natural formation in both the vegetable and animal kingdoms. in the shape of vines and convolvuli or snail and sea-shells. conjures the development of strength or condition. Its shape is to be encountered in all cultures, heavy with symbolic meaning.

NOTES

It displays the appearance of motion rotating outwards from a fixed point of origination, continuously expanding and lengthening into infinity. Its typical of those unending lines which constantly link the two ends of the future. The spiral is and symbolizes emanation. extension. evolution. cyclical but progressive continuity and rotational creation.

The spiral is linked to the cosmic symbolism of the Moos. to the erotic symbolism of the vulva, to the watery symbolism of the shell and to such fertility symbols as helix or horn. In short, it stands for the repetitive rhythm of life, the cyclical nature of evolution and the permanence of being beneath the flux of movement

The double spiral symbolizes simultaneously the two directions of this movement, birth and death, kalpa and pralaya, or the 'death' and the rebirth as a changed person which occurs in initiation. It marks the action in a reverse direction of the same power around the two poles and in the two halves of the World Egg. The double spiral is the outline of the line dividing Yinh and Yang, separating the black and white halves when their symbol is depicted. The alternating rhythm of the movement can hardly be better expressed not even by the ancient ideogram *chen*, which depicts with a double spiral the alternate expansion and contraction of yin and yang.

The double spiral is also the double wreathing of the serpents round the capuceus, the double helix around the Brahman's staff and the twofold movement of the nadi around the central *sushumna* artery ~ the polarity and balance of the two opposing cosmic currents. The same symbol may thus be expressed in the spiral's alternating rotation. now in one direction now in the opposite, as in the Hindu myth of the Churning of the Sea of Milk when the serpent Vashiki was hauled turn and turn about by *deva* and *asura*. The same is true of the bow-driven fire-stick which some have attempted to compare with the Celtic double spiral and with Jupiter's office as Lord of Fire. In Asia, drills are still used which employ very similar principles. What should be noticed in this context is that fire 1s produced in much the same way as amrita. It is the result of alternation and equilibrium between two streams of energy flowing in opposite directions. The double spiral is also related to some depictions of the DRAGON

On the other hand dragons are coiled in helical spirals around the columns of some temples, as is the serpent of the kundalint around the svayambhuva-lingam at the base of the spinal column. This is. however. An embryonic and undeveloped spiral. Yin and Yang may be regarded as sketches on the horizontal plane of the evolutionary helix. The latter continues into infinity and symbolizes the evolution and continuity of states of being — as well as degrees of initiation. as is the case in the symbolic use of the spiral staircase.

NOTES

The spiral is a lunar and aquatic fertility symbol. It is engraved upon Paleolithic statuettes of goddesses and is the equivalent of all centres of life and fecundity.

The S-shaped, counter-rotating, double spiral is a symbol of thunder and of the phases of the Moon, storms often being associated with the changes of the Moon. It expresses graphically the symbolism of fecundity associated with the network of storm, thunder and lightning and in this context may stand for the Bull-Roarer.

Many of the peoples of Black Africa regard the spiral or helix as the symbol of the dynamic of life, the movement of souls in the created and expanding universe. In this respect, the Dogon and Bambara solar hieroglyphic is most revealing. It comprises a pot (the primeval womb) around which are three (the masculine symbol) spiral coils of red copper. The latter symbolizes the primordial Word, the first utterance of the god Amma, in other words, the spirit and seed of godhead. The Bambara depict Faro, Lord of the Word, as a spiral at the centre of the four points of the compass. He takes material shape in the wicker-work hat with eight whorls which was once worn only by kings. With the spiral which he made his own when the world was set in order, 'Faro travels every four hundred years to inspect the borders before returning to the centre from which he watches over and rules the universe' (DIED). Similarly, in procreation, the man seminal fluid and his word enter the woman through her sexual organs and through her ear, regarded as another sexual organ, and coil in a spiral round the womb to make the seed of life fertile.

Further south, a similar symbolism governs the use of the spiral in the cosmogonic thinking of the Lulua and Luba, Bantu tribes from Kasai in Zaire. Souls, spirits and genii move in helical or spiral lines within the four planes of the universe. Among their hieroglyphics, a large spiral, flanked by two smaller ones, depicts the Supreme Deity creating Sun and Moon. A single spiral stands for the coiled and parti-coloured serpent which is an image of the creator and of the cyclical current of life. It also stands for Heaven and for the soul's cyclical wanderings, in succession incarnate, disincarnate and reincarnate. A spiral with its coils streaked at regular intervals signifies 'the course of human life, alternating between good and evil'. On this analogy, the shell of the giant land-snail, which is also helical and streaked, 'is an ingredient of those medicines which may be used for good or ill'.

The powerful Voodoo god, Dan, a symbol of continuity, is generally depicted in Benin in the shape of a serpent biting its tail. It is, incidentally assimilated to the rainbow and is regarded as a doubly bisexual being since it is its own twin, the two in one, 'coiled in a spiral round the world which they preserve from disintegration'. In this context the spiral clearly partakes of its basic significance

NOTES

of primeval motion, the 'creational vibration' of the Dogon, which is the basis of all created things.

Pictorially the Lulua depict Earth, Moon and Sun as a series of spirals or concentric circles, only distinguished from one another by their size or numbers. The Earth is the smallest and the Sun the largest, with respectively two spirals or concentric circles for the Earth, three for the Moon and four for the Sun.

With its dual meaning of contraction and expansion, the symbolism of the spiral is linked to that of the wHeet and is found as often or even more frequently in Celtic carvings or as a decorative motif in metalwork, pottery, coinage and so on. Modern scholarship has attempted to make it the equivalent of the Latin fulmen and a Celtic symbol for the thunderbolt, but this explanation is inadequate since the spiral is in fact a cosmic symbol. It was a motif which the Celts often carved on dolmens and megalithic monuments.

The Germanic peoples set a horse's eye, ringed by a spiral, on the Sun's chariot to symbolize the source of light.

The spiral also symbolizes the soul's journey, after death, along ways unknown to it, but leading by preordained byways to the central home of eternal being. 'I believe that in all the primitive civilizations in which it occurs, from the North Cape to the Cape of Good Hope, and in many civilizations in America, in Asia and even in Polynesia as well, that the spiral stands for the journey which after death, a person's soul makes to its ultimate destination.

There are two forms of swastikas, which are mirror-images of each other. They are commonly defined by the direction the upward arm is facing: left or right. 卐 (right-facing or clockwise) or 卍 (left-facing, counterclockwise, or sauwastika). The swastika is a symbol that is integral to the Hindu religion and has been shared with many other religions and cultures as a result of their interaction with early India. The symbol has been traced back to Hinduism and India as early as 5,000 years ago and has become deeply engrained in their society since then.

The swastika is made up of three Sanskrit roots that give reference to the good luck this symbol is thought to bring. "Su", meaning 'good'. "Asti", meaning 'exists, there is, or to be.' And "ka", meaning 'make.' When combined, they roughly translate to 'making of goodness' or 'marker of goodness.' It is commonly associated with the idea of good fortune and prosperity – so much so that it is commonly found in everyday activities. Finding a swastika that marks an entrance, doorway, or financial ledge is not uncommon. It is thought that by putting a swastika at the beginning of these things, good fortune and well-being is sure to follow. The swastika can also be found on religious texts. Such is the case with Jainism, whose texts and temples are required to contain the right-

NOTES

handed swastika.

Swastikas could be found in Roman mosaics, as evidenced in this one excavated at Lullingtone Roman Villa in Eynsford, Kent.

The swastika can be found in cultures as early as Mesopotamia, though it is most notably used by the Hindu religion. With the spread of information however, the swastika came to be a symbol that was respected by many cultures and religions.

Hinduism
Hinduism is one of the main religions that the swastika can be found in. In their religion, the swastika can be found in both the right facing and left facing design, though the right facing swastika is by far the most common. This is likely because the right facing swastika tends to be more so associated with good fortune, while the left facing swastika is associated with the tantric practices of the goddess Kali – a deity known for her protective forces that were known to leave destruction in her wake.

Jainism
The swastika is an integral part of Jainism. In Jainism, the swastika represents the four places in which the soul can be reborn in the cycle of life. These places are thought to be heaven, hell, humanity, and nature (as flora or fauna). These rebirths will eventually lead to the soul finding salvation and becoming omniscient. In the Jain religion, all temples and religious texts must contain the swastika and many ceremonies are started and ended with the sign.

NOTES

Buddhism
The swastika is also common in Buddhism where it is perceived as a symbol of the Buddha. In Buddhism, the swastika is considered to be a representation of eternal cycling – a theme that can be found in the samsara doctrine. The right facing swastika is the most common form of the symbol in this religion.

Christianity
When the Christians first came in contact with the swastika through means of trade and travel, it was adapted into their religion as 'the hooked cross.' Thus, it became another symbol of Christ's victory over the grave. In fact, some churches in modern day can be found with many swastikas in their design. This practice spans many centuries as evidenced by the painting of the Seven Sacraments by Rogier van der Weyden, in which a priest is depicted wearing a stole with swastikas in the year 1445. This painting shows the frequency with which the symbol was used to represent the cross.

Early Christian art depicts the hooked cross to represent Christ's victory over death, while a left-facing version of the swastika showed up in reference to the Norse god Thor's hammer.

[42]Caduceus: The caduceus (ⱳ;/kəˈdjuːʃəs,-siəs/;Latin:cādūceus, from Greek: κηρύκειον kērŭkeion "herald's wand, or staff") is the staff carried by Hermes in Greek mythology and consequently by Hermes Trismegistus in Greco-Egyptian mythology. The same staff was also borne by heralds in general, for example by Iris, the messenger of Hera. It is a short staff entwined by two serpents, sometimes surmounted by wings. In Roman iconography, it was often depicted being carried in the left hand of Mercury, the messenger of the gods. Some accounts suggest that the oldest known imagery of the caduceus has its roots in a Mesopotamian origin with the Sumerian god Ningishzida; whose symbol, a staff with two snakes intertwined around it, dates back to 4000 BC to 3000 BC.As a symbolic object, it represents Hermes (or the Roman Mercury), and by extension trades, occupations, or undertakings associated with the god. In later Antiquity, the caduceus provided the basis for the astrological symbol representing the lanet Mercury. Thus, through its use in astrology, alchemy, and astronomy it has come to denote the planet and elemental metal of the same name. It is said the wand would wake the sleeping and send the awake to sleep. If applied to the dying, their death was gentle; if applied to the dead, they returned to life. By extension of its association with Mercury and Hermes, the caduceus is also a recognized symbol of commerce and negotiation, two realms in which balanced exchange and reciprocity are recognized as ideals.This association is ancient, and consistent from the Classical period to modern times. The caduceus is also used as a symbol representing printing, again by extension of the attributes of Mercury.

NOTES

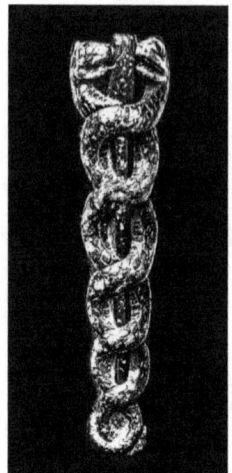

The Caduceus, symbol of God Ningishzida, on the libation vase of Sumerian ruler Gudea, circa 2100 BCE.

The caduceus is often incorrectly used as a symbol of healthcare organizations and medical practice, particularly in the United States of America, due to confusion with the traditional medical symbol, the Rod of Asclepius, which has only one snake and is never depicted with wings.

43 Staff. In symbolism, the staff appears in different roles, but basically as: a weapon, and especially a magic weapon; the support for the pilgrim on his travels and the shepherd in his wanderings; and the World Axis.

In Hindu iconography it bears all these meanings. It is a weapon in the hands of several gods, but especially of Yama, warden of the south and of the kingdom of the dead where his danda is used to punish and to keep in subjection. On the other hand, the danda becomes a pilgrim's staff in the hands of Vishnu's avatar (incarnation) as Vamana the Dwarf, and we might call it the World Axis in those of the Brahman. Ninurta's staves strike the Earth and are related to thunderbolts.

The bishop's crozier is another form of shepherd's crook. The shepherd's crook and the staff of office support the wayfarer and are badges of authority. The Buddhist monk's khakkhara supports his steps, is the weapon of peaceful resistance and signals a presence. It has become the symbol of monasticism and

NOTES

the weapon of exorcism, driving off evil influences, freeing souls from Hell, taming dragons and making the waters spring from the ground- pilgrim's staff and magic wand.

In Ancient China staves, and especially peach-wood staves, played an important part, being used at the New Year to drive away evil influences. Yi the Archer was killed by a peach-wood rod. The staff, and especially the red staff, was used to punish the guilty. In the hierarchy of a Chinese secret society, the 'red staves' still survive as ministers of justice. Bamboo staves with seven or nine knots (the numbers of Heaven) were widely used in Taoist ritual. The knots might be said to correspond to degrees of initiation. Be that as it may, these staves are reminiscent of the Hindu brahma-danda, its seven knots standing for the seven chakra, wheels, or lotuses of Yoga physiology which mark the steps in spiritual realization.

The Taoist Heavenly Masters are often depicted holding red staves. Theirs is a knotty staff, for it must show the seven or nine knots which symbolize the seven or nine doors through which the initiate must pass to acquire knowledge. Once he has gained this knowledge, he will be able to ascend into Heaven, rising by as many steps, seated on the staff held in a crane's beak. There are echoes of the Tao's journey in the legends of medieval witches riding to their Sabbaths astride a soomstick, although there is a vast difference in the sign which affects this very symbol. Generally speaking, the shaman's, pilgrim's, Master's or magician's staff is 'a symbol of the invisible steed on which he travels through planes and worlds of being.' In legends of witchcraft, the staff became 'the wand with which the good fairy changed the pumpkin into a coach and the wicked queen into a toad'.

Staves are also related to axial symbolism in much the same way as the spear. Around the World axis (brahma-danda) two spiral lines coil in opposite directions, reminiscent of the coiling of the two Tantric nadi around the spinal column (sushumna) or of the two serpents coiled round another staff, from which Hermes fashioned the capuceus. In this way, the development of the contraflow of two currents of cosmic energy is expressed. Mention should also be made of Moses' rod (Exodus 7: 812), which changed itself from rod to serpent and from serpent to rod. Some critics see this as a demonstration of the supremacy of the God of Israel, others as a symbol of the soul transfigured by God's spirit. Other writers again have regarded this alternation of rod and serpent as a symbol of alchemical alternation —*solve et coagula*. Other associations of rod (or staff) and serpent include the staves of Aesculapios and Hygeia, emblems of healing which embody the currents of the caduceus, the currents of bodily and spiritual life. They, in turn, remind us of Moses' other rod which became the brazen serpent, a prefiguration of the redemptive power of the Cross.

NOTES

From support, defence and guide, the staff became the sceptre: a symbol of kingship, power and authority as much in the spiritual and intellectual spheres as in the social hierarchy. The Field Marshal's baton, the Lord Chamberlain's staff and the rods of the Gentlemen Ushers stem from the sceptre, as their authority stems from the Crown.

The symbolism of the staff is also related to that of Fire and, consequently, to those of fertility and regeneration. Like the spear and the pestle, the staff has been compared with the phallus, Rajput miniatures being especially explicit on this point. According to Greek legend, fire spurted from the staff. Besides what Prometheus brought down from Heaven, fire was invented by Hermes rubbing two rods, one of hard, the other of soft wood, against one another. This earthly fire had a chthonian character which differed from the nature of the heavenly fire which Prometheus stole from the gods. The latter would never have become earthly unless, in the words of Aeschylus, it had descended from Olympus, the abode of the immortal Gods, to the Earth, the adobe of mortal men.

Fire, whether born of a spark, of lightning or of a thunderbolt, is fecundating. It brings rain and makes the springs overflow. When the Children of Israel rebelled against Moses because they were tormented by thirst in the Wilderness, he struck the rock with his rod and water gushed out (Exodus 17: 1-6). The priest of the goddess Demeter struck the earth with his staff in 'a ritual designed to promote fertility or to rouse the powers of the Underworld . One night, the ghost of Agamemnon appeared to Clytemnestra in a dream, going over to the sceptre which his murderer, Acgisthus, had stolen from him. He took it up and stuck it into the ground as if it had been a staff and immediately Clytemnestra saw it sprout branches and leaves like a tree (Sophocles, Electra 13-15). The staff which came alive and put out shoots foretold the speedy return of Agamemnon's son and avenger. It symbolized human vitality, regeneration and resurrection.

[44] **Nutation**: It the oscillatory movement of the axis of a rotating body (such as the Earth).

[45] **Divine Mother**: Divine Mother is a concept in yogic and Hindu philosophy that refers to the feminine aspect of the primal creator of the universe, or the spiritual spark of all life. In Hinduism, the Divine Mother may also be used as a term to refer to several of the supreme goddesses, including Adi Parashakti and Bhagavathi.

[46] **Precession of the Equinoxes:** Currently, the north celestial pole aligns directly to the star Polaris. It's also known as the pole star. This will change over

NOTES

time, and other stars will become the "North star." This is the result of the precession of the earth and moves in a circle. Precession is a change in the orientation of the rotational axis of a rotating body. The earth rotates on an axis, which can be visualised as a line through the North and South Poles, much like the center of a spinning top. This axis shifts in space very slowly, though, during millenia. On a time-frame of about 26,000 years, the earth's rotating axis seemingly describes a small circle or cone, which has been nicknamed a "wobble" in the earth's rotation.

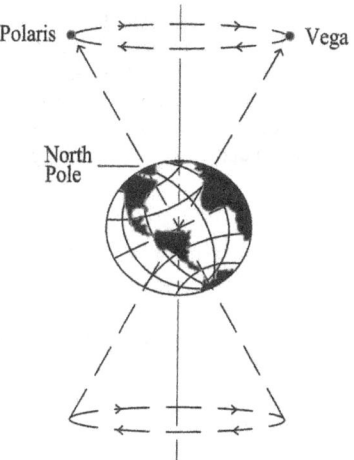

47 Flood: Symbolic meaning of the word Flood. Both Carl Jung and Sigmund Freud, the fathers of depth psychology and psychotherapy, believed that the unconscious part of the mind is the place of origin of mental images. During pregnancy, the baby is surrounded and cushioned by a fluid-filled membranous sac called the amniotic sac. When this sac breaks, it is called water breaking. Images like this one may be likened to human's life experience like birth. As a result, flood events mentioned in religion and myth around the world is a kind of collective symbology of the act of child birth. This suggests the idea of "humanity returning to the water whence it had come", and the establishment of a new era and a new humanity. Water.

48 Water. Simbolic meaning of the word "Water". All cultures naturally recognize water as a necessary source of life and survival, making it a useful symbol of creative fertility – spiritual and psychological fertility as well as physical fertility. At the same time, large masses of water are uncontrollable and,

NOTES

therefore, aptly representative of chaos – the chaos that precedes creation. Together, these two symbolic functions lead us, like the cosmic egg symbol, to the idea of potential, as yet unformed reality. The primordial waters figure strongly in creation myths from all corners of the world. The waters speak to the larger metaphor of creation as birth. We are all born of the maternal waters, and so, in creation mythology, worlds are typically born of the waters.

[49]**Universal Law**: In law and ethics, universal law or universal principle refers as concepts of legal legitimacy actions, whereby those principles and rules for governing human beings conduct which are most universal in their acceptability, their applicability, translation, and philosophical basis, are therefore considered to be most legitimate. God says that every man will reap whatever kind of seeds that he sows. This is a basic spiritual application of the first law of seeds that every seed produces after its own kind. For a example: An apple seed will produce only an apple tree and an orange seed will produce only an orange tree.

[50] **Moon**, the (planet) Lunar symbolism is to be seen as correlative with that of the sun. Its two most basic characteristics spring on the one hand from the fact that the Moon has no light of its own and simply reflects the light of the Sun, and on the other that as it goes through its regular phases the Moon changes shape. This is why it symbolizes dependence and, invariably, the female principle, as well as periodical change and renewal. On both counts the Moon is a symbol of change and of growth (crescent).

The Moon is a symbol of life-rhythms: a body which waxes, wanes and disappears, a body whose existence is subject to the universal law of becoming, of birth and death. The moon, like man, has a career involving tragedy, ... but this 'death'... is never final .... This perpetual return to its beginnings, and this ever-recurring cycle make the moon the heavenly body above all others concerned with the rhythms of life. It governs all those spheres of nature that fall under the law of recurring cycles: water, rain, plant life, fertility.

The Moon also symbolizes passing time, living time, which it measures by its successive and regular phases.

The moon becomes the universal measuring gauge .. . the same symbolism has linked together the moon, the sea waters, rain, the fertility of women and of animals, plant life, man's destiny after death and the ceremonies of initiation. The mental syntheses made possible by the realization of the moon's rhythms connect and unify very varied realities; their structural symmetries and the analogies in their workings could never have been seen had not 'primitive' man

NOTES

intuitively perceived the moon's law of periodic change, as he did very early on.

The Moon was also the first thing to die since, every lunar month, for three days and nights it vanishes as if it has died. Similarly the dead were believed to acquire a new form of existence. To humans the Moon became the symbol of this passage from life to death and from death to life and was even regarded by some peoples as the place where this transition took place, in parallel with a location below the ground. This is why so many lunar deities are at the same time chthonian death-deities like Men, Persephone and, probably, Hermes. Some, however, believed that the journey to the Moon or even life for ever on it was confined to such privileged classes as rulers, heroes, initiates or sorcerers.

The Moon is a symbol of knowledge acquired coldly, logically and in graduated stages. While the Moon, as the star of night, may conjure up metaphorical visions of beauty shining against the vast black background of Heaven, this light is merely a reflection of the light of the Sun and hence the Moon is the symbol of knowledge acquired through reflection, that is, theoretical, conceptual and rational knowledge. In this respect Moon and ow. are linked symbolically together. This is also the reason why the Moon is yin, being passive and receptive, relative to the Sun's yang. The Moon is Water relative to the Sun's Fire, cold relative to heat, and symbolically north and Winter in opposition to south and Summer.

The Moon produces water and water-creatures waxed and waned with it. As the passive source of water, the Moon is both well and symbol of fertility, identified with the primeval waters from which came manifestation. The Moon holds the seeds of cyclical rebirth and is the chalice which contains the beverage of immortality, and for this reason it was called soma, as was the drink. Similarly Ibn al-Farid made the Moon the chalice of the yin of knowledge and the Chinese saw on the Moon the HARE pounding the ingredients for the elixir of life. They believed that dew with similar properties, rained down from the Moon.

In Hinduism the 'way of the ancestors' (pitri-yana) leads to the 'sphere of the Moon'. This is not a place where they are freed from their mortal state, but they set in motion cyclical renewal. It is where finished shapes dissolve and from which undeveloped shapes emanate. This is not unrelated to Shiva's role of Transformer, his emblem being a crescent Moon. The Moon, in any case, rules the weekly and monthly cycle. This cyclic movement of waxing and waning can be related to the lunar symbolism of Janus. The Moon is simultaneously the gates of Heaven and Hell, Diana and Hecate, Heaven in this context being no more than the roof of the cosmic building. Release from the cosmos can only be effected through the solar gateway. Diana is therefore the good and Hecate the evil aspect of the Moon.

NOTES

One of the three major Chinese annual festivals is the mid-Autumn festival of the Moon-goddess Heng-ugo, which takes place during the full Moon of the Autumnal equinox on the fifteenth day of the eighth month. Offerings are made of fruit and sugar-cakes, made and sold especially for the occasion, and bunches of crimson amaranth. Men are excluded from the ceremonies. This is clearly a harvest festival and, once again, the Moon is a fertility symbol. The Moon is water and the essence of yin: like the Sun it is the home of an animal, either a toad or a hare.

Alltaic peoples greeted the new Moon and prayed for "good luck and happiness' . Estonians, Finns and Yakut celebrated weddings at the new Moon, they, too, regarding it as a fertility symbol. The Moon was sometimes taken as an unlucky sign, the Samoyed regarding it as Num's (the Heaven's) 'bad' eye, the Sun being his 'good' eye.

For example, the Maya god, Itzamna ('House of Raindrops' = Heaven), son of the Supreme Being, was identified with the Sun-god Kinich Ahau ('Lord Sun-face'). "This is why the Moon-goddess, Ixchel, was his companion and also his evil, hostile aspect, depicted exactly as he, although wearing a head-band of serpents, the attribute of goddesses'.

Since the Moon ruled the cycle of renewal on the cosmic plane as well as on the plane of Earth, together with plant, animal and human life, the Aztec lunar deities included the gods of intoxication. This was because, on the one hand, the drunkard exemplifies the cycle of renewal since when he wakes from drunken sleep he has forgotten all that has gone before; and, on the other, because feasting and drunkenness always go together and exemplify fertility since they are held at harvest-time. This is a further 'example of the harvest-rites to be found in all agrarian societies. The Aztecs called the deities of drunkenness 'the four hundred rabbits', which serves to underline the importance of the rabbit among animals associated with the Moon.

The Aztecs also believed the Moon to be the daughter of the rain-god, Tlaloc, associated with fire as well. In most Mexican codices, the Moon is depicted as 'a sort of crescent-shaped receptacle full of water over which sits the silhouette of a rabbit'. .

The Maya made the Moon a symbol of idleness and sexual laxity , as well as being the patroness of weaving, and in this context having a spider as an attribute. Also, the Moon had four symbolic meanings for the Inca. Originally it was regarded as a goddess unconnected with the Sun;
next as the women's god, the Sun being the men's; then as the Sun's wife, their children being the stars; lastly, at the final phase of their religio-philosophical thinking, as the incestuous bride of the Sun, her brother, both deities being

NOTES

children of the all-powerful sky-god, Viracocha. In addition to the primary task of ruling the skies and being the root from which the imperial Inca line sprang, the Moon ruled the winds and the waves, queens and princesses, and was patroness of childbirth.

Deification of the two great lamps of Heaven did not always result in the Moon becoming the Sun's bride. The Gé Indians of central and northeastern Brazil, for example, regard the planet as a male deity quite unrelated to the Sun.

Similarly throughout the southern Semitic world (Arabia, the Sahara and Ethiopia) the Moon is male and the Sun female. This is because night is cool and restful and the best time for these nomads to travel with their herds and camel-caravans. The Moon is also regarded as male by many settled races (soul). It guides in the darkness.

In Jewish tradition, the Moon symbolizes the Children of Israel. Just as the face of the Moon changes, so the wandering Children of Israel constantly changed their route. Adam was the first man to follow a nomadic life (Genesis 3: 24); Cain was to be a wanderer; while God commanded Abraham to leave his father's house and country.

The Moon — gamar in Arabic — is often mentioned in the Koran. Like the Sun, it is one of the signs of Allah's power (41: 37). Allah created the Moon and the Moon: pays him homage. Allah has subjected it to mankind (14: 37), especially in measuring time by means of its phases (10: 5; 36: 39) and periods (2: 185). The lunar cycle enables the date to be calculated (55: 4; 6: 96). But on the Day of Judgement the Moon will be darkened and the Sun and Moon shall be together (75: 8-9). Islam has two calendars, a solar calendar for the needs of agriculture and a lunar calendar for religious observance, the Moon ruling all canonical activities. Also, the Koran itself employs Moon symbolism, the phases of the Moon and the crescent Moon being used to suggest death and resurrection. The Prophet reflects God as the Moon reflects the Sun. The mystic, too, who has seen God's glory is like the Moon which pilgrims use to guide them through the darkness.

The Altaic Tatars can see an old cannibal in the Moon — the gods put him there to spare mankind from him — while other tribes see a hare. In central Asia, and especially among the Goldi, Ghilyak and Buryat, dogs, wolves and bears either live in the moon or are involved in myths explaining its
phases.

The Moon, its disc apparently the same size as that of the Sun, plays a major role in astrology. It symbolizes the passive but fertile principle, night, moistness, the subconscious, imagination, parapsychology, dreams, receptivity, woman and

NOTES

all that is shifting, ephemeral and by analogy with its astronomic role as a reflector of the Sun's light, subject to outside influence.

The Moon's passage through the Zodiac takes twenty-eight days and some historians believe that the Lunar Zodiac of twenty-eight houses (now obsolete in Western astrology) is considerably older than the Solar Zodiac of twelve houses — something which would explain the importance of the Moon in all religions and traditions.

Buddhists believe that the Buddha meditated for twenty-eight days under a fig-tree, that is, a lunar month or complete cycle of our sublunary world, before he attained Nirvana and acquired perfect knowledge of the mysteries of the universe. Brahmans teach that there are twenty-eight angelical or paradisal states above the human condition, that is, that the Moon exerts its influence as strongly upon the 'subtle' and superhuman planes as it does upon the material universe. The Jews link the Lunar Zodiac with the hands of the universal man, twenty-eight being the number of the word cHalal. = life, and the palms of both hands. The right hand, the hand of blessing, is comparable with the waxing Moon, the left, the hand of cursing, with the fourteen days of the waning Moon.

The Moon is the well-spring of countless myths, legends and cults, providing such goddesses as Isis, Ishtar, Artemis, Diana or Hecate with its image, and is a cosmic symbol throughout every age, from time immemorial to the present, and common to every culture.

In myth, legend, folklore, folktale and poetry the Moon is the symbol of the female deity and the fruitful forces of life incarnate in the deities of plant and animal fertility and mingled in the worship of the Great Mother goddess. Astrological symbolism carries this endless and universal stream still further by linking the Moon with the infusion into the individual of the influence of the Mother as food, warmth, love and an emotional world.

The Moon is also the symbol of dreams and the Unconscious as properties of darkness. The Dogon master of divination, the pale fox Yurugu, the only creature to know 'the first word spoken by God', which only comes to mortals in their dreams, symbolizes the Moon.

Dreams and the unconscious form part of the world of darkness. Thus the symbolism of both Moon and the unconscious associates with darkness the elements of Water and Earth, in opposition to the symbolism of the Sun and consciousness which associates light with the elements of Air and Fire and the properties of heat and dryness.

Moon and darkness could be interpreted as symbolizing the unhealthy

NOTES

imaginings which stem from the subconscious, in the meaning of 'overheated and repressive imagination'. In many different cultures this symbolism has been applied to a whole line of heroes or deities who are lunar, nocturnal, unfulfilled and malignant.

The Black Moon is an imaginary point in the Heavens and of considerable importance in astrology. It is depicted schematically as a scythe with a line through it or as two crescent Moons set point to point with a dot in the centre of the circle which they form - the unicorn's eye, a metaphysical location if ever there was one. The Black Moon is associated with Adam's first wife, ur, whose sexual organs were in her head. Basically it is linked to notions of the intangible, the inaccessible, and to the overwhelming presence of absence (and the converse), as well as of a hyperlucidity which agonizes by the very intensity of its strength. The Black Moon is something more than a hidden centre of repulsion, embodying as it does a mind-boggling loneliness and a void so absolute that it is none other than the fullness of density.

This immaterial power is also the black hole haloed by black flames which annihilates whatever it lights upon. It can, nevertheless, transfigure the astrological house in which it occurs as a birth sign, on the basis of sublimation or complete self-surrender. On other occasions, when it is the receptacle of evil influxes, disintegration is to be expected.

Hades associates the Black Moon with that dark and heavy element, tamas. It then might symbolize the energy which must be mastered, the darkness which must be scattered and the karma which must be cleansed. It is always linked to utterly opposed phenomena, veering wildly between the extremes of repulsion and fascination. Whoever is marked by the Black Moon would rather renounce the world, even at the cost of his or her own. destruction and that of others, than fail in their frantic quest for the Absolute. However, should that person be capable of transmuting its poisonous properties into healing ones, the Black Moon will give access to the 'strait gate' which opens upon such release and such light. Jean Carteret, who has devoted his studies to lights which shed darkness, emphasizes the similarities between the Black Moon and the unicorn which either destroys or divinely fecundates, depending upon whether the individual is cleansed of passion. The Black Moon denotes a dangerous path, but one which may provide a short cut to the luminous centre of Being and Oneness.

The Black Moon is the unlucky aspect of the Moon. It is a symbol of annihilation, of dark and maleficent passions, of hostile energies to be over come, of Karma, of the absolute void and of the black hole with its terrifying powers of attraction and absorption.

NOTES

51 **Shem**, **Ham**, and **Japheth** were the three sons of Noah who along with their wives were carried in the ark during the great flood. Their descendants went on to repopulate the world (Genesis 10:1). Noah fathered Shem, Ham, and Japheth after he was 500 years old (Genesis 5:32). If Noah had any other children, they are not mentioned in the biblical account. Only Shem, Ham, and Japheth are mentioned.

52 **40, Four** The symbolic meanings of the number four are linked to those of the cross and the square. Almost from prehistoric times, the number four was employed to signify what was solid, what could be touched and felt. Its relationship to the cross made it an outstanding symbol of wholeness and universality, a symbol which drew all to itself. Where lines of latitude and longitude intersect, they divide the Earth into four ortions. Throughout the world kings and chieftains have been called 'Lord of the Four Seas'... 'Lord of the Four Suns'... 'Lord of the Four Quarters of the Earth'.. by which is understood the extent of their powers both territorially and in terms of total control of their subjects doings. .

There are four cardinal points, four winds, four columns of the Universe, four phases of the Moon, four seasons, four ELEMENTS, four humours, four letters in the name of God (JHVH or YHVH), four arms to the cross, four Evangelists and so on. The Pythagorean TETRAKTYS is the product of the sum of the first four numbers (1 +2 +3 + 4). Four symbolizes the earthly, the totality of the created and the revealed.

This totality of created things is at the same time the totality of all that perishes, and it is strange that, in Japanese, the same word, shi, means both 'four' and 'death'. However, the Japanese take great care to avoid using the word, replacing it in everyday conversation by yo or yon. In the Vedas, four is a sacred number, they themselves being divided into four parts — hymns, spells, chants and sacrificial formulae. Human beings are themselves composed of sixteen parts (four squared) according to the *Chandogya Upanishad*, as is the spell for soma (comprising sixteen chants). This also applies to the instruction concerning the Brahman, which is divided into four quarters corresponding to the four domains of the universe, the regions of space, worlds, lights and senses. When the disciple knows the four quarters of the Brahman, or four times four-sixteenths, he possesses all the knowledge of his Master. Once again, then, four, together with its multiples and divisors, is seen to be the symbol of totality.

In the Bible, and especially in the Book of Revelation, four also suggests, this notion of universality, the four living creatures being the totality of all living beings in the world of light (they are covered with eyes). The four horsemen

NOTES

carry the four great plagues, the colours of their horses corresponding to the colours of the cardinal points (the two equinoxes and two solstices) and those of the day, to show the universality of their action within space and time. White is east and dawn; red, south and noon; grey, west and dusk; black, north and night. The four destroying angels standing at the four corners of the Earth (Revelation 7: 1); the four rivers of Paradise (Genesis 2: 10); the four walls of the Heavenly Jerusalem, facing the four points of the compass; the four camps for the twelve tribes of Israel (Numbers 2); the four emblems of the tribes, one for each group of three, lion, man, bull and eagle: the four letters of the name of God, YHVH, each one according to Jewish tradition corresponding to one of these emblems - Y with man, H with lion, V with bull and the second H with eagle; the four Evangelists — there could not, St Irenaeus says, have been more nor less — and each of these emblems of the tribes of Israel attributed to one of the four Evangelists and agreeing, in a most peculiar way, with the characteristics of the Gospel concerned — the lion to St Mark, the man to St Matthew, the bull (or ox) to St Luke and the eagle to St John; these creatures, furthermore, corresponding with the cardinal constellations in the signs of the Zodiac— TAURUS (bull), LEO (lion), Aquila (eagle) and aquarius (man); all these groups of four symbolize a totality.

In Ezekiel's vision (Ezekiel 1: 4ff.), dating from around 593 ac, this extraordinary symbolism may already be seen. *And I looked, and, behold. . . out of the midst thereof came the likeness of four living creatures. And this was their appearance; they had the likeness of a man.'And every one had four faces, and every one had four wings. And as for the likeness of their faces, they four had the face of a man, and the face of a lion, 'on the right side: and they four had the face of an ox on the left side; they four also had the face of an eagle*

Commentators detect the symbol of Jehovah's power of movement and spiritual ubiquity, not being tied only to the Temple in Jerusalem, but assuring his presence among the faithful wherever their place of exile. *The Jerusalem Bible* commentators also observe that the strange creatures of Ezekiel's vision are reminiscent of the Assyrian karibu (a name akin to that of the great winged creatures over the ark, see Ex[dus] 25: 18), creatures with a human head, the body of a lion, the hooves of a bull and the wings of an eagle; their effigies stood guard outside the palaces of Babylon. These servants of the gods are here shown harnessed to the chariot of the God of Israel, a vivid illustration of Yahweh's transcendence.

They also held up *a throne, as the appearance of a sapphire stone; and upon the likeness of the throne was the likeness as the appearance of a man above upon it. And I saw as the colour of amber, as the appearance of fire round about within it, from the appearance of his loins even upward, and from the appearance of his loins even downward, I saw as it were the appearance of fire,*

NOTES

and it had brightness round about. As the appearance of the bow that is in the cloud in the day of rain, so
was the appearance of the brightness round about. This was the appearance of the likeness of the glory of the Lord (Ezekiel 1: 26-8)

No better idea of God's transcendental superiority can be suggested than by this climb up the stairway of Heaven in terms of all these quaternaries.

Although more generally applied to the phenomenal world, four is again the number characteristic of the Universe in its totality. In the Old Testament both Jeremiah (49: 36) and Ezekiel (37: 9) speak of the four winds, while two visions in Daniel (chapters 2 and 7) distinguish four great periods of time embracing the whole of human history.

The number four plays a distinctive part in North American Indian philosophy and thought. It is conceived as a principle of organization, and in some sense as a potency. Space is divided into four regions, time measured in four units (day, night, moon and year); plants have four parts (root, stem, flower and fruit); there are four different animal species, those which crawl, those which fly, those which move on four feet and those which move on two; the four heavenly bodies are the sky, the Sun, the Moon and the stars and there are four winds which move in a circle round the Earth. Human life is divided into four 'hills', childhood, youth, maturity and old age; there are four basic qualities in man — courage, endurance, generosity and faithfulness — and four in woman — skill, hospitality, faithfulness and fruitfulness — and so on.

Four is also the number of completion. 'We have now made four times four circuits of the lodge ... Four times four means completeness. Now all the forces above and below, male and female, have been remembered and called upon to be with us' (from the Pawnee Hako ceremony). On the metaphysical plane, Wakantanka, the Great Mystery, is a "Quaternity [of] the God-Chief, the God-Spirit, the God-Creator and the God-Executive'. Each of these gods is himself a quaternity of two opposing dyads.

Calling to mind that Pythagoras' disciples, too, made the tetrad the key to a numerical symbolism which was capable of giving structure to the mechanism of the world.

In the Maya-Quiché tradition of the Popol-Viuh, there were four successive creations, corresponding to the four Suns and the four ages. Definitive humans only appeared in the last of these ages as Maize-Man .

Full initiation into the Algonquin Indians' medicine men's lodge passed through four degrees corresponding to the symbol of a quadripartite universe. The Great

NOTES

Manitu who presided over the fourth degree was represented by a series of quaternary symbols, among them a cross upon a four-sided pillar, each face of the pillar painted in a cosmic colour.

In Zuni Pueblo Indian cosmogony, based upon a primal sacred marriage of Heaven and Earth, Earth was called 'fourfold Earth-Mother, the container'. This confirms the worldwide symbolic quality of the number four as that of passive matter. Like the Earth, four does not create, but contains all that is created subsequently. Its property is potentiality. While four is the number of Earth, by extrapolation it may be applied to the supreme god-head, in that as the ALPHA AND OMEGA containing all things, he entrusts to Demiurges the task of creation and of bringing to life what is within him.

In addition to the four elements and the four quarters of the Earth which Pueblo Indians believed were ruled by the four rain-gods and the Maya by the four tigers or 1aGuaRs which guarded the village crops, the Zuni also believed that underground there were four caverns, the 'four wombs of the Earth-Mother'. From the lowest level and the thickest darkness in the world, came mankind, thanks to the deeds of the divine Twins, the Ayahuta warriors, created by the Sun and sent by him to look for mankind. To reach light, men had to pass through the world of soot, the world of sulphur, the world of mist and the world of wings.

The chronicler Poma de Ayala similarly states the Peruvian belief in the four mythic ages which preceded the creation of man in his present form.

To sum up, four may be seen as the sign of potentiality awaiting the manifestation which occurs with the number Five.

The Dogon of Mali regard four as the number of womanhood and, by extension, of the sun, and symbol of the primeval womb. The fertilized womb, represented as an egg with an opening in the base, an earthly replica of the intact Cosmic Egg, has the numerical value of four (top, two sides and opening in the bottom). The Foreskr is also called 'four' since it is regarded as a man's female soul and this is the reason for male circumcision.

The Dogon regard one as falsehood and uncleanness. Purity is that accuracy which demands that all created things should be two in one, the twinning achieved by the association of opposing principles. It is for this reason that four becomes the symbol of creation in the guise of its double, eight. At the beginning of time there were eight families of mankind, animals, plants and so on. However, the Dogon and Bambara regard perfection as the number SEVEN, since it brings together two opposing principles or sexes, four for the female principle and three for the male

NOTES

Among the characteristic cultural features of West African coastal tribes living between the mouths of the Senegal and Congo Rivers, are the converse sexual connotations of the numbers three and four, four being a male symbol and three a female. Such inversion is, however, exceptional.

According to Sufi tradition and that of ancient Turkish congregations of Dervishes, four, the number of the elements, is the number of gates through which the adept has to pass on his mystic way. With each of these gates one of the elements is associated, in the following order of progression: Air, Fire, Water, Earth. Their symbolism may be interpreted as follows: at the first gate (the Shariat), the neophyte who only knows 'the Book', that is to say the letter of religion, is left in the Air, that is, in a void. He is fired when he passes the threshold of initiation, represented by the second gate, which is that of the Way (tariga), in other words his acceptance of the rule of the order of his choice, those who have passed this second gate sometimes being called hermits (zahitler). The third gate reveals mystic knowledge to the man, who becomes possessed of gnosis (rif); it corresponds to the element of Water. Lastly, the man who reaches God and becomes rooted in him as in the Sole Reality (hagq) passes through the fourth and last gateway of Haqigat into the densest element of Earth. These elect are called the Lovers. The progression from Air to Earth is the exact opposite of mystic development as normally envisaged by European minds; and yet the Way of Perfection of an Ibn Mansur el Alladj or a Jalal-al-Din Muhammad Rim is not so far from that of St Teresa of Avila or of St John of the Cross. However, Sufi teachings, more clearly perhaps than Christian mysticism, postulate that what we term reality is only a reflection – and therefore unreal — of the one, transcendental and divine reality, hidden behind the veil of duality which separates the unbeliever from God and therefore places him in a state of sin. It should be observed that only one of these gateways, the second, is associated with the purifying and transforming symbolism of fire and encompasses an initiatory threshold. The stages of mystical ascension, properly so-called, are therefore only three tariga, marifa and hagiqat. This brings the doctrine very close to the three degrees of perfection recognized by the Neoplatonists of Alexandria — virtue, wisdom and ecstasy. The first degree corresponded to the perfection of social life and was attained by the practice of the moral virtues; mental contemplation acquired the second; and religious exaltation the highest degree. Such notions were the common property of pagans, such as Plotinus, and Christians, such as St Clement of Alexandria.

These four stages or gateways of spiritual perfection may be compared with the quaternary development of the anima according to Jung's theories. The analyst takes as archetypal figures Eve, which represents purely instinctual and biological relations. .. . Faust's Helen... personifies a romantic and aesthetic level that is, however, still characterized by sexual elements. .. . The Virgin

NOTES

Mary —a figure who raises love (eros) to the heights of spiritual devotion.' And finally the Shulamite in the Song of Solomon symbolized by Sapientia, wisdom transcending even the most holy and the most pure . The Mona Lisa would also represent this fourth and final stage in the development of the anima. All the same, it is patently obvious how the spiritualistic conception of the Jungian school differs from traditional mystical hierarchies.

Be that as it may, the whole system of Jungian thought is based upon the fundamental importance which he attached to the number four and he regarded quaternity as 'the archetypal basis of the human psyche' , that is to say 'the totality of conscious and unconscious psychic processes' . His entire analysis of psychological types rests upon his theory of the four basic functions of the conscious, thought, feeling, intuition and sensation. In this instance the psychoanalyst displays an attitude of mind which appears to have remained a human constant since the Stone Age. It runs from the crossed arms of the four cardinal points, a basic in all cosmogonies, through initiatory rituals and the theories of the alchemists, for whom quaternity was a fundamental axiom in the completion of the Great Work and the quest for the Philosopher's Stone.

53 Earthquakes. Earthquakes that relate to the Bible are listed in chronological order. We begin with creation and go through to the earthquake that released Paul and Silas from the Philippi prison.

1. Day Three of Creation Week

On the third day of the creation week, the waters of the earth were collected into the oceanic basins as continents appeared (Genesis 1:9-10). Before Day Three, the waters had been over the whole earth. Continents seem to have been uplifted and the ocean floor was depressed during a great faulting process that established the "foundations of the earth." We are told that angels saw and praised the omnipotent God as the earth-shaking process occurred (Job 38:4-7; Psalm 148:1-6; possibly Psalm 104:5-6). Today, the earth's continental crust (41 percent of the earth's surface, including the continental shelves) has an average elevation of 2,000 feet above sea level, whereas the oceanic crust (59 percent of the earth's surface, excluding the continental shelves) has an average elevation of 13,000 feet below sea level. Can anyone properly comprehend the colossal upheaval that formed continental crust on Day Three? Angels must have watched in awe!

2. Noah's Flood

The year-long, global Flood in the days of Noah was the greatest sedimentary and tectonic event in the history of our planet since creation (see Genesis 6-9). One of the primary physical causes of this great judgment was the "fountains of the great deep," all of which were "broken up" on a single day (Genesis 7:11). The verb for "broken up" (Hebrew baqa) means to split or cleave and indicates

NOTES

the faulting process (Numbers 16:31; Psalm 78:15; Isaiah 48:21; Micah 1:4; Zechariah 14:4). The enormous upheaval (probably associated with faulting of seafloor springs) unleashed a year-long global flood. God's purpose was to begin the human race again from the family of Noah.

3. Destruction of Sodom and Gomorrah

A disaster called an "overthrow" was delivered in about 2050 B.C. on the cities of Sodom and Gomorrah (Genesis 19:24-28). That event was so spectacular, swift, and complete that it became proverbial for the severity of judgment that God's righteous anger could deliver.5 Jesus spoke "woes" exceeding those spoken against Sodom and Gomorrah on Galilean cities that rejected His teaching (Matthew 10:15; 11:23-24; Luke 10:12). The swiftness of Sodom's judgment was used by Jesus to illustrate how sudden His return will be (Luke 17:28-30).

Of the five "cities of the plain" (Genesis 13:12; 14:8), only Zoar is described as surviving the catastrophe. Zoar is the site to which Lot and his family fled with the approval of the angels (Genesis 19:20-23). As a city, it flourished through the time of Moses and the kings of Israel, even being described as a city of the region of Moab by the prophets.6 Arab historians in the Middle Ages refer to Zoar and identify the city as modern Safi southeast of the Dead Sea in Jordan. Because Lot and his family made the journey by foot in just a few hours (Genesis 19:15, 23), Sodom must be less than about 20 miles from Zoar (modern Safi). Two Early Bronze Age archaeological sites southeast of the Dead Sea (Bab edh-Dhra and Numeira) reveal evidence of catastrophic collapse and burning along the eastern border fault of the Dead Sea Transform Fault. These two sites are likely the remains of Sodom and Gomorrah.7 A thick disturbed zone within the Dead Sea sediment core, assignable to the Sodom and Gomorrah event, occurs at a depth of about 18.5 feet.

4. Moses on Sinai

Before God spoke to Moses on Mount Sinai and gave the Ten Commandments, a great shaking of the mountain occurred (Exodus 19:18). No doubt the earthquake prepared both Moses and Israel for the important truths the Lord was going to communicate. This awesome shaking event continues to be remembered in the New Testament as the context for God's delivery of His Law (Hebrews 12:18-21).

5. Korah's Rebellion in the Wilderness

A crisis of leadership developed among the children of Israel in the wilderness (Numbers 16:1-40). Korah and all his men were killed and their possessions taken, as the land on which they were camped split apart and closed back upon them (Numbers 16:31-33). God destroyed them because they rebelled against Him.

NOTES

6. The Fall of Jericho

The wall of the fortified city of Jericho collapsed suddenly after the Israelites marched around the city seven times (Joshua 6). The biblical account does not specifically mention an earthquake, but the earth would have been shaken by the wall's collapse. Archaeological excavations at Jericho confirm that the massive wall made of mud bricks did collapse at the time of the conquest, about 1400 B.C. The site of the ancient city of Jericho sits directly on top of a very large fault associated with the Jordan Rift Valley. Surprisingly, the Dead Sea sediment core has a distinctive mixed sediment layer at a depth of 15.1 feet that is evidence of a big earthquake at about 1400 B.C.

7. Philistine Camp near Geba

Israel conquered the Philistines near Geba after an earthquake occurred in their camp (1 Samuel 14:15). Jonathan and his armor bearer were separated from their army and would otherwise have been killed by the Philistines. Is this event at 1010 B.C. seen in the thinner "mixed layer" within the Dead Sea sediment core at a depth of 13.5 feet?

8. Elijah on Mount Horeb

God spoke to Elijah at Mount Sinai (Horeb) as He did before to Moses after the occurrence of an earthquake (1 Kings 19:11). Elijah, who had been hiding in a cave, realized that the Lord does not need to use a mighty earthquake to speak, but can, in His meekness, reveal Himself simply in a "still, small voice."

9. Amos' Earthquake of 750 B.C.

The prophet Amos predicted the "Day of the Lord" (Amos 5:18-20) and a great earthquake (1:1; 2:13; 3:14-15; 6:11; 8:8; 9:1, 5). When the magnitude 8.2 earthquake occurred two years later in 750 B.C., Amos was propelled to notoriety as the earliest writing prophet at the time of the explosive emergence in Israel of writing prophets. Other prophets that lived through the big earthquake wrote about "the Day of the Lord" and earthquakes (Isaiah 2:10-21; 5:25; Micah 1:3-6). Archaeological excavations at numerous Iron Age cities show earthquake destruction debris at layers assigned to the middle of the eighth century B.C.8 Dead Sea sediment cores indicate a persistent, two-inch-thick earthquake-disturbed layer at a depth of about 12 feet in the floor of the lake. Analysis of the damage regionally indicates Richter magnitude 8.2 with the epicenter in Lebanon. That makes Amos' earthquake the largest yet documented in the Holy Land in the last 4,000 years.

10. Qumran Earthquake of 31 B.C.

About sixty years before the ministry of Christ, a small group of Levites copied Scripture onto scrolls at the small village of Qumran in the desert northwest of the Dead Sea. In 31 B.C., a large earthquake occurred along the Jericho Fault on

NOTES

the western side of the Dead Sea. The earthquake dried up Qumran's main spring and severely cracked the architecture. Spectacular evidence of the earthquake is seen at recent excavations at Qumran in cracked stair steps within the ritual baths. Grooved fault surfaces (what geologists call "slickensides") and ground rupture within lake sediment can be observed just south of Qumran. Josephus wrote of the regional devastation from the earthquake, and he said 30,000 men perished.9 The survivors buried the Dead Sea Scrolls and Qumran lay abandoned after the earthquake. The Bible, of course, is completely silent concerning this earthquake and other events during the intertestamental period. No doubt, everyone in New Testament times knew of ancestors killed in that event.

11. The Crucifixion in Jerusalem, April 3, 33 A.D.

After three hours of darkness at midday on April 3, 33 A.D., the Lord Jesus exclaimed the words "It is finished!" as He died on the cross. Immediately, the curtain of the sanctuary of the temple was torn, a great earthquake occurred, rocks were broken, and many dead saints were resurrected from their tombs (Matthew 27:51-54). The earthquake upon the death of Christ called attention to the great salvation that had been accomplished that day on the cross. The barrier between God and man was not removed by the earthquake tearing the Temple's veil, but by His Son being offered as "the Lamb of God" for the sin of the world. The centurion and his soldiers, who were given the task of crucifying the Lord Jesus, saw the sky grow dark at noon, followed by the earthquake as Christ died at 3:00 p.m. They recognized that Jesus was indeed the Son of God.

An outcrop of laminated Dead Sea sediment can be seen at Wadi Zeelim above the southwestern shore of the modern Dead Sea near the fortress of Masada. In this sediment outcrop is a distinctive one-foot thick "mixed layer" of sediment that is tied strongly to the Qumran earthquake's onshore ground ruptures of 31 B.C. (see Figure 2).10 Thirteen inches above the 31 B.C. event bed is another distinctive "mixed layer" less than one inch thick. The sedimentation rate puts this second earthquake about 65 years after the 31 B.C. earthquake. It seems that the crucifixion earthquake of 33 A.D. was magnitude 5.5, leaving direct physical evidence in a thin layer of disturbed sediment from the Dead Sea.

12. The Resurrection in Jerusalem, April 5, 33 A.D.

No human agency rolled away the stone blocking the opening of our Lord's tomb (Matthew 28:2). It was the earthquake in the presence of the angel. God's sovereign action was obvious in both the earthquake and in our Lord's resurrection. The purpose of the stone being rolled away was not to permit the resurrected body of Jesus to exit. The purpose was to allow people to see that the tomb was empty!

13. Jerusalem Prayer Meeting, Summer 33 A.D.

NOTES

Following the day of Pentecost, the assembled church in Jerusalem received the report of threats and persecution from the Jewish leaders. That compelled them to pray that the outreach of His servants and the spread of the Gospel would continue. After the prayer, the place where they were gathered was shaken by an earthquake as believers spoke boldly (Acts 4:31).

14. The Prison at Philippi

An earthquake not only released Paul and Silas from the Philippi prison (Acts 16:26), but it authenticated their testimony. The jailer who witnessed the event recognized the Lord's hand and believed in the Lord Jesus Christ. That earthquake draws our attention to how God was using His apostles to minister in the early days of the church.

Symbolism: Earthquake like Mother Earth giving birth.

54 Eight Universally eight is the number of cosmic balance. With the addition of the intermediate points, it is the number of the CARDINAL POINTS and the number of the pointers on the weather-vane of the Tower of the Winds in Athens. It is often the number of spokes in a wheel, in the rowels of Celtic bits and in the Buddhist Wheel of the Law. There are eight petals on the Lotus and eight paths in the Way, eight TRIGRAMS in the *I Ching* and eight pillars in the Temple of Heaven. There are also eight angels which support the Throne of Heaven and it is also the number — in what precise form is not known of the Mirror of Amaterasu. As the pillars of the Temple of Heaven, the angelic supporters and the octagonal plan of the LINGAM would indicate, the number eight and the octagon have also the quality of intermediation between the SQUARE and the CIRCLE, between Heaven and Earth, and are therefore linked with the intermediate world.

55 The **Maltese cross** is a symbol that is most commonly associated with the Knights of Malta (also known as the Knights Hospitallers), who ruled the Maltese islands between 1530 and 1798. The Maltese cross is nowadays widely used and associated with Malta. The Maltese cross is a cross symbol, consisting of **four** "V" or arrowhead shaped concave quadrilaterals converging at a central vertex at right angles, two tips pointing outward symmetrically. It is a heraldic cross variant which developed from earlier forms of eight-pointed crosses in the 16th century.
See symbolism of number Four. Note # 52

56 Trinity. Meaning triple, three, triad. Animals, humans, heroes or gods depicted as having linked triple bodies may stand for various triads corresponding either to attributes — the three levels of the cosmos; creation,

NOTES

preservation and destruction (Brahma, Vishnu and Shiva) - or to such properties as strength, holiness and knowledge, vitality, intelligence and soul and so on.

The components of all triads may be separately represented, but this triple-bodied depiction also indicates that below the manifold the One remains, and this is no less important than the multiform manifestation in the symbol.

One explanation for the existence in Gaul during the Roman period of many triple figures, their symbolism being related in general terms to that of the triad, is that this was the consequence of tripling their powers or multiplying their aura of majesty. The commonest religious figure of this type is triple-headed. The suggested explanation cannot, however, be the only one, for there can be no very good reason why the symbolism of a religious figure would need to be intensified. Nonetheless, both in Ireland and in Gaul, the Celtic pantheon contains sufficient members — three primal deities, three primeval druids, three war-goddesses, three Queens of Ireland and so on either with triple bodies or in groups of three, for whom some unifying explanation is essential. It is far more useful, then, to imagine three states of the same being — sleeping, dreaming and waking — or passage through the three worlds of Celtic cosmology - Heaven, Air and Earth if not passage through time. In that case, tripling would stand for the totality of time past, present and future. Triple-headed figures occur sporadically in Romanesque art, but Pope Urban VIII's decision in 1628 that they should no longer be permitted as symbols of the Trinity has meant that much of the evidence for their existence wil have disappeared.

It is important to mention as a example the triple-headed figures that of the Slav god Triglav, always depicted with three heads. This has been explained as paying homage to his universal lordship of Heaven, Earth and Underworld.

57 Infinity is that which is boundless or endless, or something that is larger than any real or natural number. It is often denoted by the infinity symbol:

58 Being: The quality or state of having existence. It is the first stage in the process by which people arrive at knowledge of the world. Being is whatever is anything

59 Circle, circumference. The Pythagoreans would say, the circle is the

NOTES

most perfect shape, it withholds all and everything emerges out of it. Every point of the circumference is the exact same distance from the center. The circle has no beginning and no end, it is infinite and stands for non-existence and eternity. The circle is, to a certain extent, the oldest of all symbols. Easier to illustrate is only a point – an that is basically a circle as well; a very small, filled one, but nevertheless a circle. Taking a closer look at point and circle we already reach the core meaning of the circle's symbolism: The circle is the outer expression, the construction; and the point is the absolute key aspect of the symbol, the core which everything turns around.

The point is like the ruling sun in astrology, it is the base from which everything exists or not. Everyone who has drawn a circle knows that this center point must exist for it's construction. This middle point stands for centralized power, the base or heart of all energy. In a transferal sense it is God, the cosmic consciousness and enlightenment. The symbol of the circle, in a general sense, stands for oneness, wholeness, unity, entity, perfection, infinity, life without beginning or end, balance and the cosmos.

In a simple way the circle shows us the complete story of creation. In the beginning there was nothing, and then there became consciousness. The consciousness is symbolized through the creation of the circumference within nothingness. We, as a part of this oneness, (consciousness) search in many different ways to find the center of this circle again. We move towards the center in concentrated circles until we bring our own reality to a point, this circulation forms a circle. Enlightenment, is the bringing together of God (the point), and the cosmic consciousness (the circle).

This is basically the symbolism underlying all circular forms and constructions, including the sphere, as its three dimensional representation, egg and spiral. All other complex signs based on circles are amplifications and variations of this ancient, prototypical symbol. Many spiritual and energetic symbols from all different cultures are based on circular constructions. Often they're seen also as protective symbols. In occult practices, standing within a circle shields people from supernatural dangers or outside influences.

he rules of the cosmic and atomic structure of many natural phenomena are based on the circular form. This alone is a good enough reason to understand the power of the symbol of the circle. I recognize a universal ground principle in this: circles within circles, in circles, endlessly – everything connected with, and within each other. An infinite mesh of concentrated vibrations.

Every thought, every form of energy, moves or concentrates in circular or spherical courses. Heat rays are spherically formed, planets circle the sun, atoms circle their center nucleus, our thoughts circle our problems, circular waves radiate in water from an object touching it's surface, etc. etc.

NOTES

Our life seems to flow in a circle. We enter the world through a circular opening, we grow up in a family circle. We see the world through a circular opening (pupils) embedded in the circular iris, which in itself is a beautiful, circular cosmos of its own.

We take our course through life and our soul leaves our mortal being through a round hole in the fontanel for the wheel of reincarnation, according to eastern religions, ... and so we experience small and large aspects of our lives taking the form of a circle.

The list of circular symbols and symbols that are based on circles is endless and would definitely go beyond the scope of this Note.

60 Infinite Law. Symbolism: Eternal Law: It represents timelessness, infinite potential and unboundedness. There is an element of limitless wisdom. For example: As an artisan conceives a project, such as a stained glass window, or a ruler conceives a law before executing it, so does God, before creating something, conceive in His Divine Wisdom the idea that will serve as a model for the being He wanted to create.

61 Aura: In spiritualism and some forms of alternative medicine) a supposed emanation surrounding the body of a living creature and regarded as an essential part of the individual.

62 Golden Rule. The "Golden Rule" is the name given to a principle Jesus taught in His Sermon on the Mount. The actual words "Golden Rule" are not found in Scripture, just as the words "Sermon on the Mount" are also not found. These titles were later added by Bible translation teams in order to make Bible study a little easier. The phrase "Golden Rule" began to be ascribed to this teaching of Jesus during the 16th–17th centuries. What we call the Golden Rule refers to Matthew 7:12: *So in everything, do to others what you would have them do to you, for this sums up the Law and the Prophets.*

63 Angels. Akkadian, Ugaritic, Biblical and other texts mentioned Angels under different guises beings who act as intermediaries between God and the world. They are either purely spiritual beings, or spirits endowed with ethereal or airy bodies. However, they can only assume a human appearance. They act as God's ministers, his messengers, guardians, steering the course of the stars, giving effect to his laws, protecting his elect and so on, and are ranked in hierarchies of seven orders, nine choirs or three triads.

NOTES

Without prejudice to the Roman Catholic belief in the existence of angels, or to the explanations of theologians of other churches, it should, nonetheless, be noted that many writers see the attributes of angels as symbols of a spiritual order.

Others regard angels as symbols of the operations of the godhead or of the relationship of God with his creation. But since opposing ideas converge in symbolism, they can also symbolize human activities sublimated, or unsatisfied or impossible aspirations. In an even wider sense, an angel symbolized 'a being in whom the transformation of the visible into the invisible which we are fulfilling, has already been achieved.' Angels with six wings, the Seraphim (literally 'the Fiery Ones') surround the throne of God. *Each one had six wings: with twain he covered his face [for fear of looking on God], and with twain he covered his feet [a euphemism for his sexual organs], and with twain he did fly* (Isaiah 2: 2). Godhead alone merits such attendants and the angels surrounding the figure of Christ bear witness to his divinity.

Angels also act as warning signs of the divine presence. To the Church Fathers they were 'the court of the King of Heaven, the heaven of heavens'. Some, who linked their beliefs to Aristotelian philosophy, believed that angels guided the movement of the stars, each being assigned to direct one star. Thus one might well enquire if the number of angels did not equal the number of stars. The mighty vault of the Heavens turned at their command and hence, perhaps through the conjunction of the stars or perhaps by more direct means, they influenced 'every plane of material creation'. They are the heralds or agents of divine intervention. According to the Psalmist (18: 9-10), these heavenly beings serve before God's throne: *He bowed the heavens also, and came down: and darkness was under his feet. And he rode upon a cherub, and did fly: yea, he did fly upon the wings of the wind.*

There is a symbolic and functional equivalence between the messengers of the Celtic Otherworld, who often appear in the guise of swans, and of Christianity's angels, depicted with swans wings, who are in any case so often messengers of the Lord.

The heavenly orders of angels are an image of hierarchical structures on Earth. Their mutual relationship should also inspire human hierarchies. This statement does not mean that there are necessarily as many angels of God as there are nations of men, simply that there is a mysterious harmony between the number of nations and the number of angels.

This harmony can change as the number of nations changes during the course of history, but it always remains as mysterious if only because the number of angels is itself unknown. The Bible speaks of one thousand times one thousand

NOTES

and of ten thousand times ten thousand: *thousand thousands ministered unto him, and ten thousand times ten thousand stood before him* (Daniel 7: 10).

Angels make up God's armies, his court and his household. They transmit his commands and watch over the world. They play an important part in the Bible. Their order is linked by their nearness to the throne of God. The three chief archangels are: Michael (dragon-slayer), Gabriel (messenger and divine instrument) and Raphael (guide to physicians and travellers). There are various views on angels. According to Justin, one of the principal writers on the cult of angels, despite their spiritual nature, angels have a body analogous with the human. Of course their food bears no relation to that of humans, since it is heavenly. In Justin's eyes the angels sin wassexual intercourse with mortal women. A child resulting from such a union was a demon. The Pseudo-Dionysius makes great play with the part angels play as enlighteners of mankind. Clement of Alexandria describes their function as guardians of peoples and cities.

The Bible makes no mention of guardian angels as such. However. according to Enoch (100: 5), saints and righteous persons have their protectors. St Basil claims that each one of the faithful is helped by an angel who guides his life and is both teacher and protector. The protective role is confirmed by the Bible in the case of Lot (Genesis 19), Ishmael (Genesis 21), and Jacob (Genesis 48). An angel delivered St Peter and St John. In the Middle Ages angels helped in time of peril and of war, during the Crusades and so on.

As a messenger the angel is always the bearer of good tidings to the soul.

64 Solgonda was the first physical contact claimed b George Van Tassel, who, according to the story, came to Giant Rock on August 24, 1953 and welcomed Van Tassel aboard his flying saucer. This served as an initiation into the secrets of the Space Brothers, out of which came his work with the Integratron.

65 George Adamski (April 17, 1891 - April 23, 1965) was a Polish-born American contactee, notably the first to gain widespread recognition for his claims to have made contact with the Space Brothers.

66 Light. *(See note # 2)*. It is commonly a symbol of life, both on earth and in the afterlife. People who have had near-death experiences will recount how they had the option to go "towards the light", which is a symbolic meaning for going towards heaven in the afterlife. In Christianity, God was said to have first created life but his first step was to create light. Light would act as the basis

NOTES

from which all life would grow and thrive. Even in non-spiritual teachings, light is said to be the source of life. In scientific theory, the light was brought about as a result of the big bang. This is said to be an expanding source of light responsible for the creation of our universe.

[67] **Prodigal** means being wastefully extravagant. In this story the man's son recklessly and wastefully spends his inheritance. In the context of this famous parable, the prodigal son has also come to mean someone who is spiritually lost and someone who has returned after an absence.

[68] **Aurora**.. Symbolism: Earth's aura. It is a natural electrical phenomenon characterized by the appearance of streamers of reddish or greenish light in the sky, usually near the northern or southern magnetic pole

[69] **Equinox**: An equinox is the instant of time when the plane of Earth's equator passes through the geometric center of the Sun's disk. This occurs twice each year, around 20 March and 23 September. In other words, it is the moment at which the center of the visible Sun is directly above the equator.

The word is derived from the Latin *aequinoctium*, from *aequus* (equal) and *nox* (night). On the day of an equinox, daytime and night time are of approximately equal duration all over the planet. They are not exactly equal, however, due to the angular size of the Sun, atmospheric refraction, and the rapidly changing duration of the length of day that occurs at most latitudes around the equinoxes. Long before conceiving this equality, primitive equatorial cultures noted the day when the Sun rises due east and sets due west, and indeed this happens on the day closest to the astronomically defined event. As a consequence, according to a properly constructed and aligned sundial, the daytime duration is 12 hours.

In the Northern Hemisphere, the March equinox is called the *vernal* or *spring* equinox while the September equinox is called the *autumnal* or *fall* equinox. In the Southern Hemisphere, the reverse is true. The dates slightly vary due to leap years and other factors.

[70] **Solstice**: A solstice is an event that occurs when the Sun appears to reach its most northerly or southerly excursion relative to the celestial equator on the celestial sphere. Two solstices occur annually, around June 21 and December 21.

NOTES

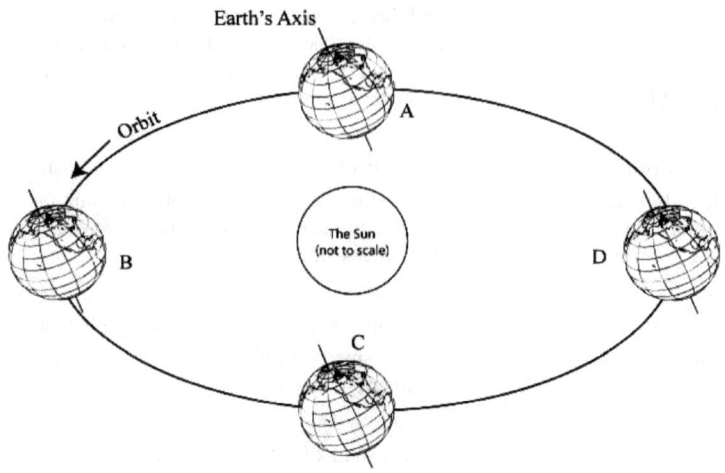

A = sept. 22/23 = Fall equinox
B = Dec 21/22 = Winter solstice
C = Mar 20/21 = Spring equinox
D = June/July 21/22 = Summer solstice

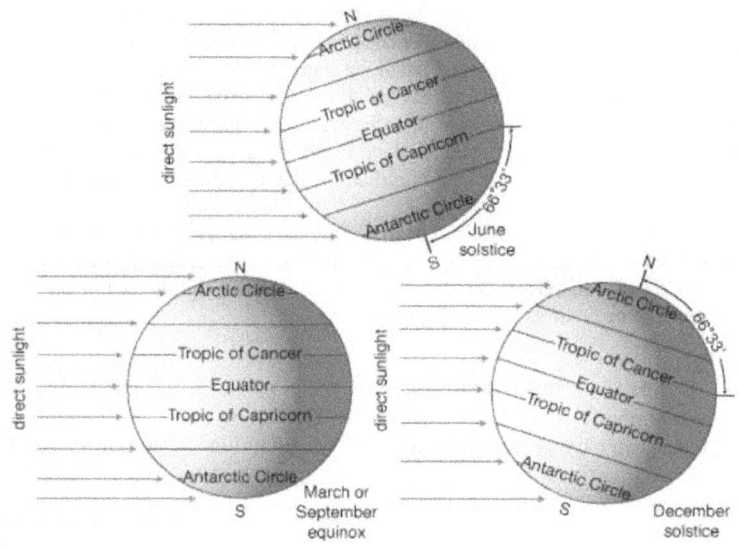

NOTES

The two solstices happen in June (20 or 21) and December (21 or 22). These are the days when the Sun's path in the sky is the farthest north or south from the Equator. A hemisphere's winter solstice is the shortest day of the year and its summer solstice the year's longest. In the Northern Hemisphere the June solstice marks the start of summer: this is when the North Pole is tilted closest to the Sun, and the Sun's rays are directly overhead at the Tropic of Cancer. The December solstice marks the start of winter: at this point the South Pole is tilted closest to the Sun, and the Sun's rays are directly overhead at the Tropic of Capricorn. (In the Southern Hemisphere the seasons are reversed.)

The equinoxes happen in March (about March 21) and September (about September 23). These are the days when the Sun is exactly above the Equator, which makes day and night of equal length.

71 6. Number 6 is the symbol of the passion of the Christ who suffered the sixth day. According to Euclid, 6 is also the first perfect number because it is equal to the sum of its aliquot parts.

72 Earth's core is the very hot, very dense center of our planet. The ball-shaped core lies beneath the cool, brittle crust and the mostly-solid mantle.

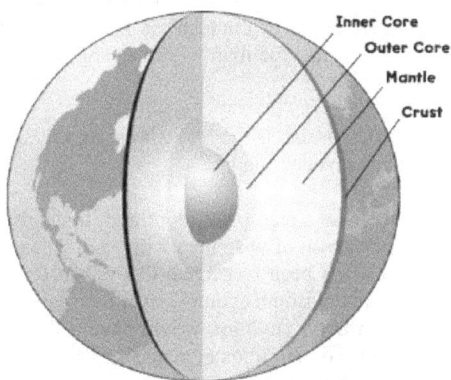

NOTES

73 Sanchea (Planet). Van Tassell claimed that he had begun to receive messages from alien beings from a planet named Shanchea. These channeled messages were directed toward the people of Earth, warning that humanity's warlike ways, in the development of super atomic weapons, threatened the peace not just of Earth, but of the solar system and beyond.

74 Star of Bethlehem. Symbolism: Planet Venus. In ancient literature, the planet Venus is often referred to as the morning star, and still is today. As far as I know, this is universally recognized. While Jupiter and Mars and other planets can appear in the morning or evening sky, Venus does so consistently and is far brighter than the others. In fact, it's so bright that on some moonless nights Venus has been known to cast shadows. Only the sun and moon are brighter than Venus. The Star of Bethlehem was Venus, the brightest star in the sky. This star guided the magi by pointing to a picture in the sky of a lion with a golden scepter, indicating the Jewish Messiah, the Lion of the Tribe of Judah.

75 Methuselah: The name Methuselah consists of two elements. The first part is מת (*mat*), which is either one of a few words to denote man or mankind, and used most often to indicate a male capable of combat, or it comes from the similar verb מות (*mut*) meaning to kill or die.Meaning: *When He Is Dead It Shall Be Sent, Man Of A Javelin.* Methuselah is the son of Enoch, who famously walked with God, and the father of Lamech the Second and the grandfather of Noah (Genesis 5:25). He is also the man with the longest life-span in the Bible (969 years).

Symbolism: Old Age. Methuselah is the one who scapes the bound of Time, the one that existed before time.A demigod.

Where old age is regarded as a sign of wisdom and righteousness -priests were originally old men. in the sense of wise men who gave guidance and where, as in China. old age has always been respected. this is because it is the image of longevity. of experience and wisdom acquired over the years, itself no more than a flawed image of immortality. Tradition would have it that Lao Tzu was born with white hair and the face of an old man, hence a name meaning 'Old Master'. Under the Han dynasty. Taoism recognized as the supreme deity Huang Lao Kun. or 'Old Yellow Lord' a completely symbolical phrase which has rightly compared with the Ancient of Days in the Book of Revelation and, one might also add. With the Druses' Old Man of the Mountains. Again in the Book of Revelation, the Word is depicted as being white-haired; yet another emblem of eternity However, <u>escape from the bounds of time</u> can find expression in the past

NOTES

as well as in the future and <u>to be an old man is to have existed before time began and to continue to exist after the universe has passed away</u>. Thus the Buddha gives himself the title of elder brother of the universe. Sometimes, and especially in the Cambodian context of Angkor, Shiva was worshipped under the name of Vriddheshvara, "Old Lord'. The Chinese secret society, Ch'ien-ti hui, is sometimes called 'the True Ancestor Society', as for example by the Vietnamese Emperor, Gia Long, in the edict in which he banned it. The 'Ancestor' is Heaven, at least for the "True Man', the son of Heaven and Earth.

[76] **Thothma**. In the *Oahsp*, Thothma is the God Thoth (*Oahspe*, Book of Wars: 25/48.14). According to the *Oahspe*, Moses refers to the builder of the first pyramid as Thothma (Oahspe, Book of Arc of Bon; 27/17.17).

[77] **Enoch** is a biblical figure prior to Noah's flood and the son of Jared and father of Methuselah. He was of the Antediluvian period in the Hebrew Bible. This Enoch is not to be confused with Cain's son Enoch (Genesis 4:17).

[78] **Vailx** in Atlantis were passenger vehicles. In the Mahabaratha, part of the ancient Vedic scriptures from India, there is also the mention of flying machines that were called Vimana. Even in certain modern Indian languages, "Vimana" still remains the word for "aircraft".

[79] 9. Number 9 symbolizes the end of a cycle or journey.

[80] 28 days. Lunar month. This period is related to fertility and birth. The average human female menstrual cycle is 28 days.

[81] **Damocles** is a character who appears in an anecdote commonly referred to as "the Sword of Damocles",an allusion to the imminent and ever-present peril faced by those in positions of power.

According to the story, Damocles was pandering to his king, Dionysius, exclaiming that Dionysius was truly fortunate as a great man of power and authority without peer, surrounded by magnificence. In response, Dionysius offered to switch places with Damocles for one day so that Damocles could taste that very fortune firsthand. Damocles quickly and eagerly accepted the king's proposal. Damocles sat on the king's throne, surrounded by countless luxuries. There were beautifully embroidered rugs, fragrant perfumes and the most select

NOTES

of foods, piles of silver and gold, and the service of attendants unparalleled in their beauty, surrounding Damocles with riches and excess. But Dionysius, who had made many enemies during his reign, arranged that a sword should hang above the throne, held at the pommel only by a single hair of a horse's tail to evoke the sense of what it is like to be king: though having much fortune, always having to watch in fear and anxiety against dangers that might try to overtake him. Damocles finally begged the king that he be allowed to depart because he no longer wanted to be so fortunate, realizing that with great fortune and power comes also great danger.

[82] **Adiphone.** This was the instrument used by Van Tassel to received message from Ashtar and other space people.

[83] **12.** Notably, twelve is the number of full lunations in a solar year, and the number of years for a full cycle of Jupiter (the brightest of the ancient "wandering stars"), hence the number of months in a solar calendar, as well as the number of signs in the Western and the Chinese zodiac.

In timekeeping:

The lunar year is 12 lunar months. Adding 11 or 12 days completes the solar year.

Most calendar systems– solar or lunar – have twelve months in a year.

The Chinese use a 12-year cycle for time-reckoning called Earthly Branches.

There are twelve hours in a half day, numbered one to twelve for both the ante meridiem (a.m.) and the post meridiem (p.m.). 12:00 p.m. is midday or noon, and 12:00 a.m. Is midnight.

The basic units of time (60 seconds, 60 minutes, 24 hours) are evenly divisible by twelve into smaller units.

In the Bible:

The 12 sons/tribes of Jacob/Israel (Gen 35:22)(Gen 42:13,32)(Gen 49:28)(Lk 22:30)(Acts 7:8)(Acts 26:7)(James 1:1)(Rev 21:12).

God promised that 12 princes would come from Ishmael (Gen 17:20)(Gen 25:16).

At Elim, there were 12 wells of water (Ex 15:27)(Num 33:9).

There was to be 12 "cakes" (loaves of bread) in the Tabernacle (Lev 24:5).

During the dedication of the Tabernacle, the leaders of Israel made an offering of

NOTES

12 oxen (Num 7:3).

The total of other offerings for the Tabernacle dedication was 12 silver platters, 12 silver bowls, 12 gold pans, 12 young bulls, 12 rams, 12 male lambs in their first year, and 12 kids of the goats (Num 7:84,87). These were brought over a period of 12 days (Num 7:78).

God ordered Moses to collect 12 rods, one from each of the 12 tribes, and place them in the Tabernacle. The rod that blossomed would be the man He had chosen (Aaron) (Num 17:1-9).

Twelve spies were sent to spy out the Promised Land (Num 13)(Deut 1:23).

Twelve stones were to be taken from the Jordan River to serve as a memorial that God had dried up the Jordan so that the Ark Of The Covenant and the people could cross it (Josh 4:1-9,20).

[84] **Infrasonic.** Relating to or denoting sound waves with a frequency below the lower limit of human audibility.

[85] **Ectoplasm.** A supernatural viscous substance that is supposed to exude from the body of a medium during a spiritualistic trance and form the material for the manifestation of spirits.

ADDENDUM

The **New Jerusalem** is called the Tabernacle of God, the Holy City, the City of God, the Celestial City, the City Foursquare, and Heavenly Jerusalem. Psalm 122 makes Jerusalem the symbol of the peace, justice and unity of the twelve tribes of Israel. It then became the symbol of the Messiah's kingdom which the Christian Church opened to all peoples.

In the description given in the Book of Revelation, Jerusalem symbolizes the new order of creation which will replace the existing world at the end of time. It no longer denotes the traditional paradise, but something which surpasses all tradition — an absolute newness.

> And I saw a new heaven and a new earth: for the first heaven and the first earth were passed away; and there was no more sea. And I John saw the holy city, new Jerusalem, coming down from God out of heaven, prepared as a bride adorned for her husband. And I heard a great voice out of heaven saying, Behold, the tabernacle of God is with men, and he will dwell with them, and they shall be his people, and God himself shall be with them, and be their God. And God shall wipe away all tears from their eyes: and there shall be no more death, neither sorrow, nor crying, neither shall there be any more pain: for the former things are passed away. And he that sat upon the throne said, Behold I make all things new. ...T am ALPHA AND OMEGA, the beginning and the end.
> (Revelation 21: 1-6).

At this point the square shape of the Heavenly Jerusalem should be emphasized. It distinguishes it from the Earthly Paradise, generally depicted as round. This is because the

ADDENDUM

latter was 'Heaven on Earth' while the New Jerusalem is 'Earth in Heaven'. Circular shapes are related to Heaven and squares to Earth. The transformation of the universe which the New Jerusalem denotes a Celestial or Heavenly City.

www.ingramcontent.com/pod-product-compliance
Lightning Source LLC
Chambersburg PA
CBHW051923160426
43198CB00012B/2009

9781736731420